Unity boosts a Community

William Doyle

ISBN 978-1-956001-59-4 (paperback)
ISBN 978-1-956001-60-0 (eBook)

Copyright © 2021 by William Doyle

Bible references taken from NKJV and NRSV

All rights reserved. No part of this publication may be reproduced, distributed, or transmitted in any form or by any means, including photocopying, recording, or other electronic or mechanical methods without the prior written permission of the publisher.

Printed in the United States of America

Contents

Foreword v
Chapter 1: The Fruits of Unity 1
Chapter 2: Learning and Earning 5
Chapter 3: Understanding Religion 13
Chapter 4: Science and Spirituality 22
Chapter 5: What we do in Time is reaped in Eternity 29
Chapter 6: Faith and Truth 33
Chapter 7: Divine Immanence 41
Chapter 8: The struggles within 45
Chapter 9: The Spirit of the Age 47
Chapter 10: Knowing ourselves 51
Chapter 11: Do our Words Help or Hinder? 57
Chapter 12: Apostasy 58
Chapter 13: Wellness Issues 64
Chapter 14: We are here 69
Chapter 15: Good and Evil 71
Chapter 16: Freedom 74
Chapter 17: A house divided against itself 76
Chapter 18: Racism 80
Chapter 19: Guidance 83
Chapter 20: Searching for God 85
Chapter 21: Reflections 87
Chapter 22: The Poetic Pedagogic Approach 91
Summary 113
References 115

Foreword

In this edition we continue to address the need for a more unified Society. Bearing in mind the restrictions imposed on the nations – due to Covid 19 - there is a need for each of us to guard against being overly influenced by mental negative impulses; these tend to weaken our resolve to be happy and contented individuals, anything less has health consequences; besides which, unity depends on me and you, if not us, then who?

We are each responsible for our own spiritual and mental growth, within our dispositions and understanding. If we do not shape our own lives, we give others permission to do it for us and in the process abrogate our own responsibilities. Furthermore, if men are not a light in the darkness, upright and honest in all their actions, communities and institutions will deteriorate and dark shadows will prevail. These influence our expressions and actions. The discerning person will guard their thoughts, which are the building blocks of human happiness and relationships. Communities and nations need revitalising; tomorrow must be better than today. Yet many people today live without firm beliefs in themselves, a Divine Creator or a bright future and increasingly experience mental traumas of various kinds. Misunderstanding about reality abounds.

There is no need to elaborate on the increasing threatening messages sent to strangers and the cyber bullying tactics, our young people have to endure. It is time for change; let us hope the impact of the Coronavirus (2020) will stir men to adjust and face the realities confronting humankind.

The Divine Books of the Ages all point to the message of love, tolerance, compassion, charity and unity. Yet no one can deny that satanic cruelties continually make their ugly presence felt across the nations, invading our space. Unless and until men are prepared to seek the truths outlined in the world's spiritual literature and be guided by higher consciousness, disunity will continue; but we can change all that, when our own inner world experiences a measure of tranquillity, our outer world will be more settled.

William Doyle

1

The Fruits of Unity

The fruits of Unity will ripen when the peoples of this world accept that all forms of life co-exist for the mutual benefit of all and the enrichment of the local environment in which they live. The principal reason why these benefits are slow in maturing is because of the emphasis on competition, not cooperation, together with negligence of Natures laws and animal welfare.

The earth's ecosystem is basic to all of life and human growth in particular, an interconnectedness threads its way through the entire creation process; it cannot flourish completely if even a segment is misused, injured or destroyed, e.g. the photosynthesis of plants is essential to human life. Earth's foliage must be protected and communities made aware that we shall not nurture or preserve planet earth if we do not address these issues, with thoughtful, intelligent care.

Each individual has a responsibility to care for the land and all other ecological treasures, not only for ourselves, but future generations. This is the challenge before us; shall we rise to it and thwart any disintegration? We alone are responsible for the way we treat the earth. We do not want to run the risk of being labelled its aggressor, if it isn't cared for. The earth is our home for the time being, when men understand the reason why the earth is here and humankind are on it, for a while, they will realise we are its carer, not its oppressor. Quite naturally human beings seek enjoyment and some go to great lengths to achieve it, exploring the avenues of wealth, power, sex, drugs and the ideals of self-realisation, among other things, only to discover dissatisfaction and often despair.

The sacred writings show how God wants His children to live in the love and excitement of peaceful and helpful relationships, free from division, confusion and hurt. But all too often strife enters relationships, weaving havoc and leaving wounded souls, alienated from one another. Men often find themselves in a dark place and behave accordingly.

The ancient teachings point to a way of enjoyment in this life, which is through an infusion of love, cooperation, integrity and unity; this naturally guides us into one central purpose - communion with God and helping our fellow human beings. Often the dark shadows of the mind prevent this from happening. We need to be aware of what motivates our decisions. Each of us have to live in this world with all its ramifications. In this respect, the spiritual path is no easy option and never has been. Truth is, life is hard and we have to face up to it and face the issues intelligently, justly and honestly.

Early believers were warned not to make friends with the world; this is *enmity with God* (James 4:4). This world was created to be enjoyed and for people to live peacefully together. Granted the temptations of the world will draw us away from all that is wholesome. Good and evil walk side by side, but we don't have to hold hands!

When through the mouth of the prophet, our gracious God urged Jeremiah to tell the people *to seek the ancient paths, where the good way is and walk in it ... the people said, we will not walk in it* (6:16). Much the same is happening today; because God never takes away our power of choice. If He did we would cease to be morally responsible and we are not puppets!

It takes a courageous soul to obey God for it means that through our obedience we may enter a period of desolation; God is not beyond testing His servants. Many of the saints and mystics experienced years of frustration until the *morning star arose within their hearts* (2 Peter 1:19). God always leaves a way out of the shadows into the light.

An integral part of our life on this planet, is our thanksgiving and praise for all the blessings God has bestowed upon us. We praise Him for who He is and out of this attitude, flow the prayers of gratitude. God has bestowed many blessings on the human family, fatherhood, motherhood, childhood, home, and friends and so on. The blessings of God are an outpouring of His overflowing grace and benediction and not granted to us by merit. There may come a time when cares and worries increase, problems seem to mount up, these are signs pointing us to our 'prayer closet.'

> *Do not be anxious about anything, but in everything by prayer, and petition, with thanksgiving, present your requests to God* (Philippians 4:1-13).

This is our first port of call when the storm threatens; prayer turns inner turmoil into outer peace. As the human soul matures and we recognise the will of God in all our affairs, we more easily express our gratitude for the Gift of His Spirit and experience a joy that lifts us up in times of need, for *every good and perfect gift comes from above* (James 1:17).

There will be those who say, people are satisfied without God and many believe that to be true, but this satisfaction is a surface sensation only; e.g. their views satisfy their present understanding. Whilst we may be content at being happy and enjoying pleasure, it is not the same as experiencing joy. Happiness depends on what happens, joy does not. The miracle of the spiritual life is that we can experience joy even when surrounded by misery. This in turn enables us to work towards a solution until the gloom is removed.

Joy comes to us as we get rightly related to God and follow His Messengers or in today's terminology, the 'Manifestations of God.' These enlightened Beings showed the Way by doing the will of God on earth; when we follow Their lead we discover that happiness is in the taste of things, not in the things themselves. All young people are entitled to their happiness, but as we mature and experience the stern issues of life we come to realise how much we are in need of God's grace. The only sure way of finding enjoyment in this present order of things is by remembering that 'our chief aim is to glorify God and enjoy Him forever.' We are accepted in the Beloved through what Christ and God's Messengers came to do, namely to educate our minds, understand ourselves and encourage us to follow God Will.

2

Learning and Earning

As we learn, so we earn, this is not a reference to money with which to acquire things, but knowledge, especially when we make it our own. The lazy mind attains very little. We are each responsible for our development and maturity; we learn from our mistakes, or repeat them. Be not of those who remain oblivious of unreality and continue on blindly. Witness the behaviour in the warring communities, the social misbehaviour in many nations, the unwise conduct during the height of the Coronavirus, by some. Unless and until we come together in unison, pool our resources, express goodwill towards neighbour and work so all may benefit, none shall prosper, as they would wish. No one is immune to the trials of life, the wavering of the economy, or the effects of thoughtless infringements of Nature. We rob ourselves of the treasures of the Kingdom of God by our diversity and lack of understanding of our creaturely nature.

Common sense urges the unity of peoples and nations. Indeed, unity of the 'whole of creation' forms part of the Divine Plan for all humankind. In the Torah the patriarch king David, (approx. 1035 - 970 BCE), rejoiced that it was *'good and pleasant for the brethren to dwell together in unity ...'* (Psalm 133) and ever since men, from all walks of life have called for law and order, yet it continues to allude the nations.

Through the centuries sentient beings have expressed warring intentions and at the same time an attitude of independency. This dangerous assertion among men, takes the form of deceptive thinking. Furthermore, the eschatological view, denominationalism and sectarianism eats at the fabric of unification, depriving the community of prosperity. In the meantime those who are concerned with ecumenism should have no argument with the maxim, *ubi Christus ibi ecclesia*, 'where Christ is, there is also the church,' pointing to the church as being *in* Christ, rather than in any sociological or cultural organisation. The church is called to deliver God's message, in truth and in love; to praise His glory in human relationships.

Significant steps towards unifying God's people have been attempted, some have succeeded, others have wavered, or failed; but we continue to find a way. One of the problems that prevent the followers of the different religions from unity seems to be one of identity, which results in churches cherishing their independence. This is not a criticism of any church or religion; but we suffer a delusion when we think that independence makes us strong, it does nothing of the sort, it merely shows up our unrealised weakness. The Lord Jesus was not independent of 'higher authority,' His life was one of complete submission to God.

Christians, under the guidance of the Holy Spirit and common-sense can do much to penetrate the ecumenical impasse that has thwarted developments towards uniting God's people and do so in a spirit of love. The unity of the church is after all grounded in the saving work of God in Christ. If people will pause and think, a way will be found that is 'illumined by the light which shineth in the darkness, even though 'the darkness comprehendeth it not' (John 1:5).

Bringing the churches together need not deny their origins and customs; to my mind it opens the way for more cooperation leading to the universal gathering of all people under the banner of Christ. It is not the will of the All-Glorious Deity that there should be separate families under God. Every effort should be made to heal the divisions between Jew, Gentile and the different denominations. Believers worship and honour the One true God. The same can be said about the so-called 'separated' Christian brothers and sisters, divided from mainstream churches; it is time these 'broken fragments' were brought together and embraced in the name of the Christ of God.

It is also time to forget those activists who have previously persecuted Jews and break this vicious circle; also for Gentiles to recognise that the New Testament is for Jews, as much as it is for Gentiles. It is true that many Jews do not accept Jesus as the Messiah, even though the Gospel is relevant to them.

Jesus was a Jew, born of a Jewish Mother, He grew up among Jews; His closest friends and disciples were Jews. If all peoples put aside their prejudices and searched their hearts, they should find no real objection in following the teachings of Jesus and accepting Him as the Messiah, since His life and everything He taught is noble, honest and a saving power. Indeed the constant message of the Bible is that people need to be saved and God provides salvation. Furthermore, God invites each person to discover their wholeness and freedom in a close relationship with Himself; He also guides them from the place where they are, to the place where they are destined to be. Indeed, the main theme of the Gospels is that God will deliver humankind from the misery of sin.

Morality and human happiness are inseparably linked with salvation for everyone, whether Jew or Gentile. God's salvation plan, unfolding itself in history has a *unity* which was determined by The Deity from the beginning and which was to be consummated in Christ. The Messiah Himself explained this point to two of His disciples:

> *... how foolish and slow of heart you are, so unwilling to put your trust in what the prophets have declared ... then beginning with Moses, He interpreted to them the things about Himself in all the scriptures* (Luke 24:25-27)

The prophets have proclaimed that Christ is the cornerstone of God's community (Isaiah 28:16; Psalm 118:22; Matthew 21:42; Ephesians 2:20). He is sought after by Gentiles as well as many Jews (Isaiah 11:10; Acts 10:45) It was Jews who brought the Gospel to non-Jews and St. Paul, the chief emissary to the Gentiles was used by God to accomplish this.

There is one God; if we fail to come together in unity under the banner of the Christ, how shall we fulfil God's command: *'to love one another as I have loved you'*? Though there are differences among us, we stand together with vision and joy under the banner of His Christ, healed by the Lord and worshipping Him. This is the privilege of every generation throughout the ages, during which time God sent a Prophet to enlighten the peoples on earth and remind them of God's edicts. The fact that each Messenger was treated harshly confirms the ugly nature of men and their inability to recognise goodness and truth, even when it is staring them in the face. Albeit, the minds of men have improved, yet there remains among the populace a segment, who doubt and misunderstand. A broad Spiritual Education will appease this situation in the course of time.

In the meantime the challenges and changes we experience in society today calls for a fresh look at human attitudes, personal faith and discipleship. Humans are life-long learners, seeking ways to grow, improve and change (hopefully) under the guidance of the Christ Spirit; it's a two way partnership. The prophets in the OT were always challenging the people to move out of their comfort zones and follow Yahweh. In our time change is often forced upon us as the economy ebbs and flows. In all communities, fortunes change, social conditions, things and bodies change, the climate changes; all this is in keeping with the cycles of life, to which we are subject, e.g. hot and cold, night and day. However, the year 2020 has seen new challenges with the impact of Covid 19 which has caused many painful experiences. The prophets of old warned of difficult times ahead and advised: '*Be still and know that I am God …*' Yet men continue to war and cause division; the sound advice of the wisdom contained in the Sacred Books of the Ages and common-sense is ignored, so the world must face the consequences.

To close this chapter, we do well to remind ourselves that we are living in times when the Deity is often disregarded and not consulted in the deliberations and affairs of men. If divine assistance is ignored and God's designs continue to be rejected or an attempt is made to change them, dark clouds of deception will continue to form in the minds of many.

There is clear evidence that more and more men no longer view Nature as sacred, showing that Divine influence is in the world; the corollary is that instead of collaborating with the beauty of nature, men desire to be her master and not content in brutal oppression, expect sub-sentient lives to serve human needs. It is time to wake up! Our community leaders and indeed the church must stir itself and take responsibility. Clergy have a duty to proclaim the true Gospel message, assisting people to walk in the light of the Christ principles. For too long now the Church has allowed the world to influence her behaviour. Many years ago a man of God – Jeremiah - living in Old Testament times said this:

> *Woe to the Shepherds … who scatter the sheep of my pasture* (Jeremiah 23:1).

These words from the prophet Jeremiah to God's people of his day, constitutes a warning for many of the clergy of this generation. It doesn't take a prophet or a theologian to see that such woes will descend on the church of today if these words are not heeded; indeed those clergy who fail to be what they're called to be, risk calling these woes on themselves and the whole Church will suffer more deeply.

The clergy in particular have a duty to makes clear their high calling and teach and safeguard the Faith, to care for the people and live in such a manner as to adorn the Gospel of Christ, the Chief Shepherd of the sheep. It is clear that clergy are no longer in the forefront of community activities and relationships to act as spiritual teachers and mentors, as they once were. The activities of parochial clergy is largely unsupervised; Orthodoxy has been redefined to make its content significantly less than it has been in the life of the Church over many centuries. Thus the 'woes' prophesied by the prophet Jeremiah remain a threat.

What applies to the shepherds of the established churches, applies to all the people, for all have a share in the ethos and content of the spiritual life of humanity. Woe to these shepherds and under-shepherds. The woes will fall on all of us; already we see many churches closing, apostasy growing, and unbelief spreading like a rotten apple! With many unsuspecting souls being influenced by charlatans; people in the pews appear to be in a deep sleep, unaware that any peril exists! We've become intoxicated by our own ideas, opposing the Voice of the Lord, but this cannot continue for much longer. Will not the Lord of all creation allow woes to fall? Is not the world weary of resistance and apathy, coldness and inflexibility, especially when it comes to assemble for unity?

The Church is imploding because of division, clamour for diversity and the abuse of some clergy towards younger colleagues (Curates). This behaviour can be halted when repentance and forgiveness is exercised;

when the human ego is kept in check and all embrace the Lord Jesus Christ in all His glory and holiness. If not, the woes will increase.

How many people are starved of spiritual nourishment? How many experience the shadows of uncertainty because of the failure of shepherds to care for the flock, for which Jesus the Christ died? It is time that a unified, clear and unambiguous portrait of godliness, sound teaching, good and decent order was made known. Regrettably, far too many clergy seem ruled by their own ideas and passions that fail to adorn the Gospel of Christ.

Having made these observations, there are many clergy in our churches who genuinely care for the flock and continue to minister lovingly by biblical standards, with little thought of career prospects, concerned only with promoting the kingdom of God on earth; we thank God for them. However, what is clear is that if the decline in the church-way-of-life is to be halted and is to survive as a godly form of the one, holy, catholic and apostolic Church, then the shepherds (bishops) and under shepherds (priests) must turn about and preserve the true faith, guide the sheep towards increasing the scope of the mind and heart, raising the personality to a greater spiritual awareness, otherwise there will be an increase in secular forces occupying their field. Yet even that can be halted when the church shows more influence in the world and doesn't allow the world to change the church, for seeds sown here are reaped in eternity. Work towards purifying heart, renewing the mind and Truth emerging from where it has always been, will guide our thoughts and actions.

A fresh approach to education

The English novelist, George Eliot (Mary Evans) has said: "aesthetic teaching is the highest of all teaching because it deals with life in its highest complexity..." Teachers, teach your students to see the picture as well as the diagram and you will not only have informed their minds, but instilled in them a seed that will mature in the course of time. Imaginative literature may not be 'diagrammatic' but can be seen as nurturing the human spirit. Granted the diagram is perhaps more descriptive, but with the picture there is freedom for personal response and interpretation; a good example is Holman Hunt's picture of Christ 'at the door' which has no handle/latch.

I'm sure you've already discovered that our assumptions and presuppositions often influence our reading of certain phenomena – hence religious texts are interpreted differently – though it should be acknowledged that 'Variation theory' promotes the idea that variation is necessary to learning.

3

Understanding Religion

A contributing factor towards unity in the community is more easily achieved by closing the gap between the different religions; having an improved understanding of our own makes us more toleraance towards others. There is, after all, only One God and Him we serve.

An all-inclusive form of Religious Education (RE) is much needed. RE motivates the pursuit of religious knowledge and traditions, this may lead the aspirant towards a spirituality which has vital links with human behaviour. RE is a relevant issue because it affects the choices people make and the experiences they have in life. The educational significance of RE reveals that an understanding of Christian, Muslim, Bahá'í and other religious core beliefs, enhance not only our own knowledge, but leads to an improvement in the spirituality of the individual, which in turn motivates human behaviour for good and affects the thinking processes and the choice of decisions made. RE also opens avenues to a greater awareness of our true selves. No one can live beyond what they believe. Any neglect or efforts to consign RE to silence will rob generations of people to a propensity for relationships. Teach the value of all true religions and Unity will more easily prevail.

Each adherent of the different religions are called to follow and obey God's Divine Will and live the teachings to the best of their ability. For followers of Jesus one of the finest examples is Mary the Mother of our blessed Lord; she did not hesitate to subject herself to the Will of God. Most fair-minded people honour this holy lady and rightly so; it would also narrow the gap between Christians if all men joined together in celebrating the birth and life of our Lord's Mother, as a gesture of love, for someone whose heart was pure. This is not to advocate a worshipping attitude towards Mary as we do her Son. She of all women would discourage that. The irony is that men worship idols on earth, but not God's Messengers.

Long gone are the days when women were 'kept in their place' or had no voice in public affairs; thank heaven that attitude has changed, at least for the most part in the Western hemisphere. Did Jesus not select a woman – *Mary Magdalene* - to be the first missionary? Did God not raise up patriotic women, among them *Joan of Arc*, 'The Maid of Orleans' and *Deborah* who became a judge in the land and ably assisted the Army General Barak in battle? (Judges 4:4-24). Who can forget *Tahirih* (1816-1852); a remarkable devout Persian woman, born into a rich, prominent family and excelled in knowledge of Islamic studies and poetry, (unusual for a woman at the time). She was considered beautiful, intellectual, articulate and fearless, wanting only to serve God and His chosen messenger, known as the Bab. She embraced His teachings and the coming of the promised One with courage and went on to spread the message, saying: 'Let deeds, not words be our adorning' (Nabil. 1932:286).

Attending a meeting, mostly of men, Tahirih removed her veil, causing shock and surprise to the whole assembly. At one conference she is reported as saying: 'When will you lift your eyes towards the Sun of Truth?' Her strong faith in the new teachings brought disapproval and she was sentenced to death. When the hour came, she called out: 'You can kill me ... but you cannot stop the emancipation of women.' Tahirih sacrificed her life for the cause she believed in, all of which she had foreseen in a dream.

There were many godly women who have made a difference; under the command of God's Edicts, these women stung the enemy. Conversely the different denominations today are stinging God's children, wounding and keeping them apart. It is time to end this travesty and unite all God's people.

Every generation finds some new revelation in the sacred scriptures; it is not that the message has changed, because God's Word does not change. But every so often God sends a fresh Message to earth through His chosen Prophet for the edification of the people. These revelations come to light because man has matured spiritually and is able to discern the truth of what is written, which had previously been veiled from their sight, mostly by symbolic explanations. For instance the return of Christ has long been misunderstood. Even the disciples close to Jesus did not understand everything their Master had told them. When asked: 'When will the kingdom of God come?' Jesus the Christ answered, '... *Behold, the Kingom of God is among you.*' (Luke 17:20). It is so today, were men aware of it.

Another misconception that arises is that when Christ returns, He will come in the clouds:

> *'Then will appear the sign of the Son of Man in the heavens and all the people of the earth shall mourn as they see Him coming in the clouds of heaven with power and glory ...'* (Matt. 24:30).

Can the clouds of earth support the weight of a human being? I think not. These verses have an altogether different meaning. A literal interpretation will take the reader off course. The use of the word 'cloud' in scripture symbolises our limited knowledge, e.g. *'Moses went up a mountain and a cloud covered the scene … for six days; on the 7th day the Lord called Moses out of the midst of the cloud* (Exod. 24:15). Moses came down from the mountain more enlightened than before He ascended to meet the Lord. Both the Lord and Moses were hidden by the cloud, meaning that His coming may be obscured by the clouds of our imagination or lack of knowledge. Seeing anything of a divine nature calls for spiritual vision; the message cannot be descerned by rational thought alone.

One of reasons human eyes are veiled from observing the divine Ground of the divine Message is because we have become bogged down by the old paradigms, without questioning them; e.g. it is known that the body replenishes itself and once it has recovered from a time of depletion it is restored to some form of balance. On the other hand some physiology does behave badly, as Anne Harrington has described in her book: 'The Cure Within' (2008:250). In it she records the desperate plight of some women in Cambodia forced to witness the torture and killings of their loved ones, which caused them to go blind, though medics found nothing wrong with their eyes and since ageing forms part of the human condition, this too must be considered in our search for the divine understanding. On the other hand, when one becomes ill and feels well cared for they are more likely to recover, a principle that has been known since the first physician took the Hippocratic Oath.

Unless and until, the rich help the poor, the strong assist the weak and all receive an adequate education, we shall not progress as custodians of this earth, our temporary home. Education reduces and eliminates poverty, opening up opportunities for work, increasing the realisation that all learning leads to knowledge of God. In the process young people can learn to avoid religious extremism and a narrow-minded approach to science; seeking reality at all times.

Throughout the ages, all the Messengers of God have counselled men thus and called them to service, to honour God and each other, to recognise the oneness of humankind, to show unity and love, regardless of race, creed or colour. It is pivotal to human progress. Let no one think they are excused from doing their part. When there is less competition and more cooperation we shall have matured and be more prepared for the next step – improving our spiritual nature. A new light will then dawn upon the world and strengthen the foundations of our endeavours, preparing the ground for a more enlightened civilisation, which was planned long ago.

In the dispensation of Moses, the prophet Malachi asked:

'Have we not all one Father? Hath not one God created us? Why do we deal treacherously every man against his brother, by profaning the covenant of our fathers?' (2:10).

Likewise, in the Qur'an the Prophet Mohammad declared:

'An Arab has no superiority over a non-Arab nor a non-Arab any superiority over an Arab; also a white has no superiority over black nor a black any superiority over white, except by piety and good action …' (Islamic Quotes: compiled by Muhammad Imran).

The message of the Bible is not a programme of social improvement for a fallen world, nor is it a literary critique to satisfy the intellect; but *Salvation* through FAITH in God's Edicts. Men find this a stumbling block, because they have been blinded to the truth, which is clearly laid out in Scripture (see Isaiah 9:6; 1 Tim 3:16; Titus 2:3; Luke 1:47; John 10:30 and 20:28).

We pray that the Spirit of the Living God will take the veil from our eyes, since all the time we are divided and experience different church denominations, this will weaken the ties of unity. To grow strong all must unite and lay aside man-made theologies. It is worth repeating, unity among Christians, Muslims, Baha'is and others, will encourage spiritual growth which is declining in various nations.

Until we can live in peace among ourselves and all men are guided by higher principles of behaviour, there is a need for Shepherds and Shepherdessess. Some call these 'End-time apostles,' men and women imbued with pure souls, empowered with the Holy Spirit, not authoritarians ruled by egoist tendencies, but the love of God, which whether we are Jew or Gentile, we cherish and wish to emulate. Such individuals exude a light that will brighten our path and guide us aright. In its absence the enemies of Christ have taken it upon themselves to wage war on the Gospel message and on all who follow holy, spiritual teachings; even in this enlightened age there are nations who continue to persecute and kill Christians and Baha'is.

In these 'end–times' God's people will have to be alert to the increasing dangers facing them, such as deceptive false teachings, apostasy and the watering down of Gospel truths. The rebellious and hostile behaviour we witness in society indicates the urgent need for God's Message to be more widely known, so that more people can decide to seek the Holy Spirit and so bring about the changes that will enable them to hold firmly to the love and beauty of genuine spiritual teachings, since the age we live in is presenting greater global threats to humanity. Those who make international policy have a duty to give serious attention to the reality of these obliterating risks.

It is not only religious people who are concerned with the destruction of life and the planet. Decent people from all walks of life have expressed concern about the possibility of the end of the world as we know it. From a Christian point of view the world will end, but as God defines it, though men may hasten its demise! However, it does not take a theologian to see that this present time of human rule on earth is under deceptive influences (1 John 5:19).

A fundamental problem that all humans share is the inner battle going on between the flesh and the spirit; the scriptures allude to this (Galatians 5:16) and of course no one escapes its infringements, it affects everyone, whether we're conscious of it or not. The spirit and the flesh are contrary forces, one prevents the other doing the things we ought to do. This teaching from the Apostle to the Gentiles points to the flesh being at war with the Spirit and the Spirit with the flesh. When the soul acts without counsel or influence from the spirit, the outcome falls short of all God intends for the wellbeing of His children. This to my mind is partly responsible for the problems facing society today; we ignore it at our peril. However, it follows that all the time we are in this physical body, we shall experience a struggle between the flesh and the Spirit within us. The only escape, as Paul explains, is to *walk in the Spirit*. We do have a choice, pray God we choose wisely.

All higher sentient beings are constantly caught up in this spirit/flesh battle, so Paul gives us a divine formula. He says, when we walk in the Spirit, we are not under the Law; the law he is referring to is the Law that guided the early Israelites, i.e. the Law introduced by Moses, to guide the people in the OT. It was these laws the Pharisees of old were hell-bent on preserving. Paul is saying that Gentile Christians are not under the Law of Sinai. This law was given because of the people's transgressions; it was a good law at the time and was made for the lawless, the ungodly and profane.

NT Christians believe we are under Grace, brought to us by Jesus through His sacrificial death. Paul confirms this and teaches that, *sin shall not have dominion over you, for you are not under the law but under grace* (Romans 6:14).

More people have been brought low because they have held thoughts of doubt and remorse, dwelling on past wrong-doing, but the fact is the law can only demand good conduct; grace inspires and creates it. Yes, we may have *sinned and fallen short of the glory of God,* but the way through this moral maze is a metanoia – a true repentance - the rest is God's work. By harking back to past sins, trying to please God, we unwittingly place ourselves under the law; but when we are led by the Spirit we shall not be under the Law. This teaching makes no reference to the laws of the land; we are obliged to obey those! On the other hand we are mistaken if we think we can please God by pleasing men; this only causes frustration. We please God through faith, with the help of the Holy Spirit. So Paul says, those who have the Spirit are not under the law.

Paul was a man of privilege, having received the best education available at the time; he knew something of the law. Indeed, he followed it to the letter. His life was devoted to upholding it and anyone not complying with it felt the wrath of his office; but God turned his passion for the law into a desire to serve Him and carry the divine message to the Gentiles. Paul was able to do this because he subjected himself to God's will, as he constantly reminds us in his letters. He served Christ and not men; nothing else existed for Paul but God's love and so he was able to be an unhindered witness for Christ. This apostle was gripped by the love of Christ, which is why he acts the way he does; he abandoned himself completely to His Master.

You may recall the children of Isaac had failed to recognise the Messiah; the children of Ishmael had mistaken the identity of the Son of Mary. The Book of Genesis tells the story. Indeed, it is a sad story of jealousy, anger and division; the 'shock waves' of what happened are still being felt today. This lesson preserved in the Epistle makes clear that the

Apostle Paul was intent on urging men to be aware of the Judgement Seat of God and the Love of Christ. Read it for yourselves with the eye of discernment, for as surely as the sun rises in the morning, we shall face this divine reality and our eyes and heart will be opened to the truth.

4

Science and Spirituality

A deeper understanding of scientific principles and spirituality, more easily answer the questions we have relating to ourselves and discover the peace and enlightenment we seek, which inevitably leads to unity in the community. Our belief system is important in our lives, reasoning and faith are essential guides, leading us to a measure of fulfilment, education, love, joy and understanding. Lack of knowledge leads to impoverishment; no one can be happy when feeling a sense of emptiness within, which more often than not only God's Divine Grace can fill. Besides the fruits of spirituality we need science and commonsense to guide our steps; these provide a light that guides us to reality.

Prayerful reflections on spirituality and the scientific aspects of life, as we know it, draws us away from the lower mundane self to the higher consciousness, where the mind searches for enlightenment, answers relating to the forming of the Universe and knowledge of our true nature.

A study of the cosmos has become known as *Cosmogeneses,* a word which makes reference to the creation of the universe and how it came into existence; it is a subject which profoundly affects everyone, even if people do not understand all the issues.

Whether we look out into the cosmos or peer into the living cell, we are conscious of harmony and order; to get the most from it we do well to read and understand it with the eyes and the mind of the spiritual self. It is not necessary to have a scientific or religious education to know that heat can cook or kill or that there is a First Cause, known as The Absolute, The Uncreated One, A Universal Designer, which humans call God.

Science rests its case on the intellect and explains only what it knows; our religious faith is not based on the intellect, but on a relationship, through which knowledge is conveyed to open minds and teachable, receptive spirits. Since both science and spirituality have a profound effect on every individual, it is imperative that there is some understanding of both. God has called His people to seek knowledge, before they perish (Hosea 4:6). So I write not to undermine the work of scientific specialists, or become embroiled in religious dispute, but to encourage enquiry from alert, discerning minds.

The Relationship between Science and Spirituality

Science sets out to prove on the validity of the reasoning faculty what is observable; spirituality on the other hand, encourages the pursuit of truth and a relationship with God who cannot be seen, but is attainable through His Messengers. The quest for truth is a form of worship and implies faith that the universe is a cosmos, not a chaos. In other words, it is susceptible to mental images and the orderly arrangement of things is a feature of mental activity. Since there are laws governing every aspect of life and the universe we do well to work with them. However, God has done what the law cannot do (Romans 8:3). Humans seek God, as water seeks its own level; therefore the conclusions to be drawn from the modern picture of the universe point to a Divine Creator, in whom believers put their trust.

Everything in the universe consists of atoms on which the universe is assembled; they are the stuff of life and have within them a guiding intelligence, yet we cannot think of them as solid stuff at all; perhaps they are best thought of as manifestations of energy – vortices in magnetic space-time. Hundreds of thousands can sit on the point of a pin. The atom consists mostly of space filled with magnetic fields. Science shows that if these atoms are split, the core or nucleus of the atom releases enormous energy. Atoms combine in intricate patterns to form molecules; compared to an atom, a molecule is the size of a house. Yet the cosmos is homogeneous and the human mind can be seen as the final product of an on-going Infinite process.

The Living cell

A living cell is a beautiful complex piece of precise engineering. It has a central nucleus surrounded by cytoplasm in a membrane. In the cytoplasm energy is located producing plants of the cell; the nucleus of the cell contains the blueprint – the genetic code – for its own production. Some cells hold the genetic code for a colony of cells. A single cell may be regarded as a factory equipped with tools and production lines. In each cell complicated chemicals called enzymes, work together to achieve chain reactions. In cell-division rod shaped chromosomes appear, divide lengthways and separate in opposite directions; the rest of the cell divides into two cells. The nucleus then becomes normal again. It is all wonderfully accomplished by a Genetic code contained in the DNA (deoxyribonucleic acid) molecules of the chromosomes. Sometimes there is interference with the DNA and a distorted message is sent out, causing the multiplication of rogue cells which result in disharmony in the body, leading to illness of varying kinds. All this complicated interchange of chemical codes takes place in a space almost infinitely minute and is extremely difficult to translate into everyday language. However, when science and spirituality become closer allies, science should recognise that the force behind everything is the Energy and Great Spirit of God. See (Psalm 33:6; Colossians 1:16; James 2:26; 1 Cor. 3:16), for affirmation.

A Living faith

As we move forward on our journey of exploration, we find that faith develops the certainty that God is behind everything. The old cosmology of Genesis and the miracles of the New Testament may not stand up to the light of modern scientific knowledge, but think of it this way: Miracles are the symbol – the language of religion. Mathematical equations are the symbol – the language of science. In a continuum it is not possible to conceive of anything being present which was not in some form always present. Why should the dust of the cosmos manipulate itself so that it comes to control the very stuff of which it is made? To put it in simple language, the only reasonable explanation is that a Supreme Mind has breathed into chemical dust the 'Breath of Life.' How else could God speak to a human being, except through another human being? The *Logos* 'became flesh' and dwelt among us, so that mind could exercise a measure of control over the cosmos and be guided by the will of God.

In our present state the mystery of life is insoluble. Science explains what it knows and what it knows and expounds has evolved from the religions of the world, defined in the Divine Books of the Ages, which teach that life and mind are supreme manifestations of God's creative love; it is in the Christ Spirit that love will be fulfilled; then will come the spiritualising of humankind, making manifest the spiritual love which

Christ urged upon the world, the seed of which is in the heart of every woman, man and child.

Metaphysics

The study of metaphysics has an important role in our understanding of life, it reveals all that is good and positive in all the religions of the world and our comprehension of their teachings. The founders of all the religions were endowed with great humility and exciting spiritual gifts, endowed by God; they were reliable Guides and an inspiration to the people of their time, their wisdom speaks to us today. Each of these great spiritual leaders gave themselves tirelessly to the divine plan for humankind.

Each founder of every religion spoke and acted from their culture. Those who followed tried to capture the heart of the beginning and the soul of the founder, so they could carry the message into the future. Institutions and structures grew out of their efforts. What started out as one person caring for another or a man in search of his God became a creed to be spoken and rules to be followed. Sacred sites where founded and became tourist attractions. However, the one singular point that was overlooked by many, after their establishment, was that is there is only one God and one Divine plan; over a period of time icons and false beliefs replaced reality.

The religions that have evolved on our planet have spawned a number of atheists, as well as many believers. Individuals, once keen eager explorers for the truth began to think they knew better than their founding fathers and God who inspired them. Some decided this is the way of God and this is what we shall do. As a result many have turned away from God and are reversing God's design or attempting to do so. There is little appetite for exploring the spiritual path. Atheist and believer are caught up in this merry-go-round. Once a person thinks he knows the truth, he no longer explores, but defends his faith. He joins with others and finds safety in those who believe as he does, in creeds and dogma that reinforce the truth he thinks he knows; though not all those who were of the faith are without merit. Many are loyal and trustworthy. They provide a place to test new ideas, providing a path to improved understanding, showing the Meta way is a better way, which benefits all.

Here in the West metaphysics is seen as the study of the fundamental nature of all reality – what it is and why; how we are to understand it. On the other hand, another view widely held, is that metaphysics is seen as the study of 'higher' reality or the 'invisible' nature behind everything, although this is slightly misleading. We would be closer to the truth if we referred to it as the study of all of visible and invisible reality. Unless one has experienced a higher state of Spiritual Consciousness within oneself and integrated that Awareness into one's conscious daily life, that person has no true foundation from which to teach or comment on spiritual truth.

Many obstacles stand in the way of creating the life we want for ourselves; these can include fear, doubt, lack of belief in the idea that we can succeed or having a poor opinion of ourselves, even to attracting ill-health; e.g. minor epithelial tissue irritations on the scalp, or other areas of the body which reveals itself as a manifestation of an outward sign from inner frustration. We choose to believe in all or any of these weaknesses that form in our character and personality, which often affect our mental and physical health.

Human weaknesses side-track or hold us back from achieving what we really want in life. In effect we are expending energy in the wrong direction, thinking and acting out of weakness, not drawing on the Source of energy that sustains and harnesses our success-drive mechanism that exists within us. If we have faith and believe in ourselves and are ready to yield our will to Divine Law, we should succeed in eliminating any weakness that stands in the way of our success, marching on to achieve mastery over other weaknesses we may have accumulated.

5

What we do in Time is reaped in Eternity

The sacred Books of the Ages all agree on unity among humankind, e.g. in the Book of Psalms (133:1):

> '*Behold, how good and how pleasant it is for brethren to dwell together in unity! It is like precious ointment upon the head ...*'

In the NT, '*above all put on love, which binds everything together in perfect harmony* (Col. 3:14).

'*By this all people will know that you are my disciples, if you have love for one another*' (John 13:35).

'*O mankind! We have made you into nations and tribes, that ye may know each other, not that ye may despise each other*' (The Qur'an 49:13).

The Herald of the Bahá Faith, wrote: '*Is there any Remover of difficulties save God? Say: Praised be God! He is God! All are His servants and all abide by His bidding!*'

> *'So powerful is the light of unity that it can illuminate the whole earth'* (Bahá'u'lláh, Epistle to the Son of the Wolf, p.14).
>
> *'When religion shorn of its superstitions, traditions and unintelligent dogmas, shows its conformity with science, then will there be a great unifying, cleansing force in the world which will sweep before it all wars, disagreements, discords and struggles and then will mankind be united in the power of the Love of God* (Abdu'l-Bahá. Paris Talks, p.146).

Since the time of Moses, in the OT, the Almighty God has sent numerous Prophets and Messengers, from the East, for the express purpose of guiding His people, enabling them to know their Creator and attain His presence. In our times, these nations in the East, once the glorious flower of creation, have sadly descended more and more into conflict and chaos. Indeed, all creation is in travail, waiting to be delivered from the vanity of men and *time*. As day and night divides our time, so good and evil divide our thoughts, words and actions. Whether we are conscious of it or not, we are agents of one or the other and we shall be carried along with our choosing; whatever we do in *time*, shall be reaped in *eternity*.

Clearly a spirit of deception and delusion has been loosed on the nations (2 Thessalonians 2:10-11). People are calling good evil and evil good. But *'Woe to those who call evil good and good evil ...'* (Isaiah 5:10). These sentiments continue to be practised today as more and more people "*hate the good and love the evil*" (Micah 3:2); yet there is a remnant that is loving and law abiding. However there remains a perversion of justice and truth in our communities; the more clearly the truth is told, the more firmly it is rejected. We see evidence of this further afield; events in the East, Europe and elsewhere are taking its toll. Are we so blind that we cannot see - what happens to one influences all!

People who voice views of holiness or speak up against the madness of war and other contentious issues are ridiculed and accused of intolerance. Dark rhetorical shadows are attempting to cover the light of truth. The prophets of old foretold this time of deception years ago, can we not see it? The enemies of Truth are active, whilst many lovers of God are sleeping!

The messages of the prophets are for the ears of the inhabitants of the earth, but who's listening? These Messengers of the Deity have revealed God's amazing deeds for human benefit and are not to be taken lightly. Yet not-with-standing the gentle patience of the prophets, the nations do not understand what their end will be, as they continue to mistreat God's people. The prophets echoing God's Will says, 'Vengeance is mine … and recompense for the day of their calamity is at hand.' The Book of Hebrews repeat the early prophets warning, '… *The Lord will judge His people*' (Heb. 10:30-31).

The prophets have always made it clear that the Creator God is very much involved in the affairs of this world through established Divine Laws, though men have free will to organise and manage them. Little imagination is required to realise that if divine assistance is ignored and divine designs continue to be rejected or an attempt is made to change them, dark clouds of deception may well form in the minds of men leading to confusion. In planning their worldly ventures, men fall short of the success they might have achieved had they invited God into their deliberations.

The age we live in seems be uncomfortable with the term, 'God.' Perhaps it has something to do with the influence of the Old Testament, where one learns of God's wrath. Monotheists see the Deity as a *God of Love*. If we believe that God does get angry, we should not see it as the anger of men, they are not the same. Angry men are impulsive, careless, uncontrolled. The anger of God comes with full prophetic warning and leads to a blessing. God is not vindictive, as men are.

Science has now come to accept what mystics, metaphysicians and monotheistic religions have long believed, that our lives and the universe are subject to Divine Law – these are our guidelines for living this life. When these Laws are fractured or violated, there is a price to pay. No one is immune from their influence; all forms of life, vegetable, animal and human, are subject to them, hence all forms of prejudice is foolishness and a violation of divine law. There is much evidence too of an increase in materialism, with people failing to heed the prophets call. Many others steeped in their religious beliefs, have not taken time to be sure their views are correct; still others are sucked into the secular Babylon of our times.

The peoples of the world will make greater progress when all desire unity with each other. The human family is one and just as the many coloured flowers add beauty to any home garden, so the different shades of human skin provide splendour to the gathering of human society; all of whom are God's Creation and subject to His Love and Divine Law.

6

Faith and Truth

The word *faith* has a variety of meanings, which we do well to distinguish. Some consider it as *trust*, others as *authority*, having belief in what someone says because of their special position in society, such as lawyer, physician or theologian. On the other hand, there is a faith which is an act of the intellect moved to assent by the will in matters of science, though the principles behind it may not be understood. Faith is a precondition of systematic knowing. Then there is *religious* faith, which justifies and saves. However, one must be aware of its downside. In its extreme, it can be uncompromising and dangerous; hence one is wise to seek truth in matters of belief.

Faith

Most of us experience moments of uncertainty, times of unknowing, a crisis in faith, it happens to the nicest and brightest of people. Faith in the NT is a means of understanding the Christ Spirit is within us, giving us unshakable confidence in the God of all the worlds. If we have trust, only in His power to act when disaster strikes, we may lose faith when God seems to do nothing. There is much that looks like the power of

God which isn't, so we must have faith and confidence in God no matter what happens.

Faith is not a mathematical problem. When bad things happen we need to believe that God is good and that He loves us in spite of all that contradicts our experience. There are times in our lives when the truths of the Gospel and rationalism come into conflict; we may have faith in good management and good common sense, but who among us has faith in our Lord Jesus Christ when things do not go the way we expect, even after doing what we believe to be right?

We drive ourselves to distraction by trying to understand why bad things happen and God remains silent or appears so. We don't live by 'Murphy's law,' but by God's law. There is purpose in the Cosmos and the Infinite Mind is greater than all creation.

So much is accomplished through faith, for instance in agriculture the farmer endures the hard work involved only because he believes he will reap a harvest. He may or may not be familiar with the words of the Teacher in Ecclesiastes but he abides by them and sees results -

> *Whoever watches the wind will not plant; whoever looks at the clouds will not reap* (11:4).

If any man was credited with wisdom, it was Solomon; his advice is that *the race is not always to the swift ...* (9:11), we do well to heed his words; so many people drive in the fast lane for so long they find themselves in the rat race! Our faith may have to endure great trials, indeed there are some things that are learned only in the 'fiery furnace,' but the more we hear God's Word the greater our faith becomes (Romans 10:1-17).

During our lifetime we shall meet all kinds of disasters; who can make sense of the loss of a baby, the flooding of homes and towns and the damage done by earthquakes, these things challenge our faith, but that's the nature of faith, it will be tried and tested; we must be prepared. We cannot make sense of human tragedies unless we have an unshakable faith in a higher power - God. The proof that we have a vigorous faith is that we express it in our daily lives and are willing to testify how it came about; reading and listening to sacred scriptures is the surest way of strengthening our ability to do so.

As we explore God's Word with a prayerful mind, hope is nurtured, faith grows and the light of the Son of God in us attracts ministering angels to guide and inspire us on our path. The brightest pupil in school, the most learned professor, may have faith in their ability to work out complicated theories and problems, which make him/her stand out among the crowds, but faith in God does not rely on the intellect, indeed the high intelligence with which these gifted people are endowed may prove to be a stumbling block to faith in the eternal God in Christ. Why? Because the head insists on employing rational thought to unravel spiritual matters, as it does the secular.

Many people have discovered a faith late in life, even at the moment of dying; before they died they experienced such love and devotion to the Christ Spirit, their fading consciousness at death lost its sting to cause pain and bitterness. The Christ makes death sweeter for those who love and trust in Him. Indeed, our faith in God has its own reward, so let us not give up; however small our faith is, it may become the means by which God unveils His purposes to us.

If we say we have no faith, it's because we are not in touch with the Lord of Life; get in touch with the Christ Mind and lack of faith disappears. In matters of faith we so often employ the old pagan ways, we use the head and not the heart. *God looks on the heart*, not on our merits.

Of all the stories of faith told in the OT, the one recorded in the book of the prophet Daniel, about three young men sentenced to death for refusing to worship false gods (golden statues) is most poignant; as these young men stood facing the blazing furnace into which they were about to be thrown, certain they would burn to death in the flames, they told the king, *even if our God does not rescue us, we want you to know, O king, we will not serve your gods* ... They did not put their confidence in God's deliverance, but in the goodness and love of God, as a result they were saved and the heathen king turned to the one true God (Daniel 3:13-30). Their story has been repeated by many Christians, Baha'is and others who demonstrated a love of God. We may not be called to face such tests, but if are going through a crisis of faith and there remains a strand so small, even to the *size of a mustard seed,* God will take hold of that and our flagging faith will be restored. However, most people can speak eloquently of their time in the wilderness - the place of desolation - where tests and trials have taken their toll. These are of varying degrees and are dealt with according to the skills and innate disposition of the individual. No matter how skilful we are in overcoming the hurdles facing us, the actual experience can often be painful. The importance of these challenges and the accompanying temptations cannot be underestimated; our deadliest enticements are not those that destroy our beliefs, but those that corrupt and destroy character.

Truth

The perennial question of *truth* has challenged countless minds for centuries. The theological perspective is that it is based on faith as 'conscious knowledge' and adopts a belief in a Divine Source or Revelation; a process through which the unseen God makes Himself known. The philosophical outlook takes its viewpoint from critical thinking, the pervasive use of reason as a tool for understanding reality. Whoever perceives the truth of the words uttered so long ago: I AM

THAT I AM, will never fall for deceptive ideologies, so prevalent in these times.

When investigating truth and other profound issues in life, one shows wisdom if they think the issue through for themselves, since philosophy itself cannot serve as the standard of truth, nor can it offer any pragmatic solutions to the ills of society, because it lacks some degree of validation. For truth to have meaning, it must be real and express itself in its purest form. Unadulterated truth is a gift of the divine grace of God, enabling us to see that it is verifiable. Indeed, the thoughts of the foremost Prophets of God, reveal the purest form of truth, in both their words and in the lives they lived, showing the theme of God's religion to be the unification of all people. When this truth is discovered by the clergy, community, national and international leaders and all people, we shall have set in motion the elements for improving this world for the generations who will follow and the truth will gently be revealed, as a garden rose slowly unfolds, revealing its beauty.

In our search for improvement we discover that without a measure of suffering little is achieved in this world. Do not fear the ravenous fire, it must shed its burning light. In the exhausting fires of sorrow, we yearn for release. Maintain hope and courage, soon the distress will cease. It is when we are blinded by the attractions of materialism that humankind misses the reality that would have further enriched their lives. But even now it is not too late. When people get their house in order, turn to God's Messengers and their teachings in the Divine Books and do so without reserve, we shall have discovered that a panacea for the world's ills was present all the time; but since men, by and large, have failed to recognise this jewel of civilisation, God continues to send His Messengers at different times throughout history to assist the advancement of humanity. Their message assists all humankind. Be not of those who ignore these gems of knowledge.

We learn from their study that a truly spiritual religion is less concerned with external influences; rather it relies more on the seeker's inner attitude and desires to nurture it. The influence of rational thought, whilst building up an arsenal for robust discussion and debate, tends to cast a mental shadow over the spiritual scene, making it less easy to sense the one-ness we have with each other.

The Christian term, 'antichrist' or the 'son of perdition' i.e. the dark side of the human mind, is responsible for much of the evil atrocities witnessed in society. The Quran also recognizes that 'The evil eye is real …' Buddhism teaches, 'There has to be evil so that good can prove its purity above it.' The mind of the Antichrist believes itself to be omniscient and rejects all Universal Law attributed to God and anything resembling the Deity. Hence the 'Antichrist' hates prayer and the noble virtues of faith, courage, hospitality, truth, industry, patience and humility. The human mind is programmed to think on these things, but has chosen to absorb less spiritual concepts, which to my mind results in negative and sometimes destructive behaviour.

Another contributing factor to consider is that much grief has been caused by thinking other religious practices are wrong or their way is the only way to salvation; this has resulted in a drive to convert others to their own faith. True religion is not about changing other people, but changing ourselves and becoming one with the Infinite Intelligence of the Universe – God; in my view this opens the mind to spiritual avenues, leading to improved understanding of other great religions in the world. When we omit the desires of self, we discover the divine Ground.

The wisdom teachings reconcile all religions, at the same time does not deny the Deity. Do the rays of the sun not form part of the sun itself? We each have to decide which of the world religions portray the One true Infinite, Unknowable God and not the gods dreamed up by men. By all means let us recognise the outstanding spiritual leaders for the wonderful truths brought to humankind; each One was a divine Messenger, who brought wisdom from on high. They proved to be able transmitters of truth and knowledge, showing a 'picture gallery of Eternity.'

The fruits of a spiritual life are shown in the way people live their lives. Spiritual guidance seeks to mellow the human ego. Until men recognise that the various denominations and the religion they promulgate are branches of the same tree and that true religion is an expression of the love of God, men will travel their own path, remain separated and miss the true Way which the divine Messengers of God have demonstrated in Their teachings; e.g. when facing the 'Tempter' – which monotheistic religions call the devil - we do well to remember that the lower aspect of the mind, from which evil actions spring, is not much impressed by the wrong things we do; its most cunning weapon is to get us to lose what God has put into us by *regeneration i.e.* spiritual rebirth.

When the Christ Spirit enters our soul, we have an overwhelming love of God, yet almost at the same time, we can expect a surge of opposing forces; on the other hand, it puts us in a place where we can be of value in God's service. The worldly mind doesn't think much on these spiritual issues, but it is just as important to be concerned with the soul, as it is with our bank balance and since it is not uncommon for some hacker to steal our bank details, let no one think they are immune from those who would use subtle techniques to lure us away from our spiritual bank account.

The increasing influence of materialism is taking captive the imagination of many unsuspecting people; it may be classed as our Babylon. It is as if the 'Tower of Babel' is being rebuilt again, only this time in computer technology, which is fast becoming an invitation to flirt with the dissemination of our culture. What started out as a useful, informative, communicative, entertaining device, is now being used by unscrupulous individuals to convey their evil intent; bringing unsavoury scenes and comments into our homes. We have to be careful we do not get carried away with these trends and not allow them to sway our good intentions, nor interfere with our true purpose in life.

We cannot always protect our children from what Shakespeare calls the 'arrows of misfortune,' though it is the adults duty to warn every child not to allow the vicious comments of cruelty and hate, so often portrayed in the 'tweets' and discussion groups of modern communicative technology, to enter their own thinking. This simply escalates and destroys inner peace.

The message of the Christ was very simple; He advocated the victory of love, compassion and faith over orthodoxy, all of which points to a new world order, including the realisation that humanity is one. We are connected by virtue of our physical and spiritual nature. Brother is called to support brother. Until we acknowledge this fundamental unity we shall go on as before, which has brought us to the place where we are now.

More perception, compassion and obedience is required, but this calls for a spirit of humility. Without obedience men tend to go it alone and become self-centred and rebellious, a god unto themselves; it is this attitude that has contributed to the problems facing society today. It happens I believe, chiefly because men are living outside the authority established by God. The person who has learned to obey God's line of authority will count themselves as nothing and they will be entrusted with more. Then shall dawn on the minds of men the unutterable beauty of God's word.

May God who knows how we struggle to keep our faith and endeavour to discover the truth, strengthen us daily and help us to know that He is present when the clouds descend, as He is in our triumphs.

7

Divine Immanence

Divine Immanence is a truth stated in all the sacred Books - God dwells in His creation and is indivisibly present in all His works - This is not meant to imply Pantheism, which describes God as the sum of all created things; nature and God being identical. The term does not do justice to the glory of the incorruptible Deity.

The *Infinite Presence* is a fact. God is here and expresses Himself through His Spirit and communicates with us through the avenues of the mind, our will and our emotions, yet it is essentially through the spirit that we sense Him. However, there are various interruptions to human awareness, leading us to overlook or miss entirely the divine presence. These may be attributed to the seeds of decay in Western Society which has increasingly emerged in public life and which we often unknowingly absorb.

TV programmes seen by millions portray lascivious images and prurient mass entertainment. Little wonder faithlessness and decadence is on the increase. Thus the prophesies of the OT seers are seen to be true:

There will be a time of distress …' (Daniel 12: 1). 'The new wine dries up, vines sicken, revellers turn to sorrow

> *... no one shall drink wine to the sound of song ... mirth is banished from the land ... this is how it will be in every nation'* (Isaiah 24:7-13). *'...the earth will reel to and fro like a drunken man'* (Isa. 24: 20).

In numerous nations many have abandoned spirituality and faith, all in the name of enlightenment and progressive values. There is an urgent need for people to renew their faith and love for God and neighbour.

When society was in its nomadic stage, as tribes or groups wandering through deserts, fields and mountain terrains, each group had a religion of their own. Later when these tribes settled and became nations, religion took on a national character. Yet the teachings of these religious Founders were not written down until some years after their formation. Nonetheless, the wisdom in the Holy Books have provided a haven for people down the ages and all are free to inhale the perfume from these Garden of Delights, which each of the Books have to offer. One only needs to inhale the perfume from these celestial gardens on earth, experience freedom from attachment to things and surrender to the Beloved; then shall the lives of all men have moved a step nearer to refining the human character and unifying the human race.

Reading Spiritual literature awakens the seed of eternal awareness embedded within each human being and reveals the oneness of humanity; an issue promulgated in the Bible and taken up again afresh, by the emerging Bahá'i revelation, indicating the continuity between the religions, e.g. the Hindu Faith made way for the Zoroastrian and Buddhist Faiths, the Jewish Faith – with the advent of the Christ Jesus - gave birth to Christianity. The Islamic and Bahá'í Faiths have great affinity and speak highly of Christianity. None of the Founders ever criticised the teachings of the other, yet each One was a Reformer Himself and revealed something new, during His dispensation; showing He was part of a grand redemptive scheme.

Religion impacts our lives; yet true spirituality is waning in our society. Exercising a spiritual outlook is generally born of love, sacrifice, suffering and much prayer. A more intimate knowledge of the *Shepherd* and sound biblical exposition is required to feed the minds of the people if there is to be a revival of the spiritual life and a joyful desire to serve humanity.

The Holy All gracious God is deserving of our praise. He put His Spirit within us so that we can recognize Him and respond to His love. How much longer shall men resist His Spirit? A body cannot live without a heart. Christ's Spirit is the is the sweet manna from heaven nourishing our souls. Happy are those who open their hearts to His Spirit and blessed are those who believe in Him. Yet is not this generation guilty of apostasy. Is it not true that some of our spiritual leaders question the fundamentals of the faith? We need to return to a simple, childlike faith in Jesus and a greater trust in God. History reveals the outcome of those nations who do.

When prayer and the Fruit of the Spirit are absent in the minds of men and community, ominous clouds darken our space and in some men dire misbehaviour is committed. The world is at spiritual crossroads, men need to decide if the holy words of God are real and what they are going to do about it. Are we as a society of intelligent, creative people going to place ourselves under the pastoral staff and banner of the Heavenly One or go our own way?

Who can deny that the light of the true knowledge of the Christ Spirit is faint in the hearts of men? There is an urgent need, in these days, for the human heart to turn to God and be enlightened by His Holy Spirit and show a genuine response to Him in worship, repentance and faith. God's covenanted blessings, which include revelation to a true

Divine Immanence

perception of divine realities remains available, yet men tend to draw away from God. They no longer see creation in a holy way and the Gospels as the Word of God. Men are losing the desire and a longing for the blessed Christ Spirit, many others are unaware that the Kingdom of heaven is within them bringing to fulfilment all He has taught.

8

The struggles within

All the time we are in this shell we call the physical body, we shall experience pain and inner struggles. In the Christian text this tension is referred to as adverse pressure between the flesh and the Spirit; the only escape, as the NT teacher Paul explains, is to *walk in the Spirit*. We do have a choice.

All of us are constantly caught up in this spirit/flesh battle, so Paul gives us a divine formula. He says, when we walk in the Spirit, we are not under the Law; the law he is referring to is the Law that guided the early Israelites, i.e. the Law introduced by Moses, to guide the people in Old Testament times. The Pharisees of old, were hell-bent on preserving these laws. Paul is saying that Gentile Christians are not under the Law of Sinai. This law was given because of the people's transgressions; it was a good law at the time and was made for the lawless, for the ungodly and profane. The laws of the nation in which we live are to be obeyed; pray they are fair and just, not oppressive.

More people have been brought low because of holding thoughts of doubt and remorse, dwelling on past wrong-doing, but the fact is the law can only demand good conduct; grace inspires and creates it. We may have *sinned and fallen short of the glory of God,* but the way through this moral maze is a metanoia – a true repentance - the rest is God's work. By harking back to past sins, trying to please God, we unwittingly place ourselves under the law; but when we are led by the Spirit we shall not be under the Law. This teaching makes no reference to the laws of the land; we all have to obey that! On the other hand we are mistaken if we think we can please God by pleasing men. This causes frustration; we please God through faith, with the help of the Holy Spirit. The apostle Paul says, 'those who obey the Spirit are not under the law.'

Many obstacles stand in the way of creating the life we want for ourselves; these can include fear, doubt, lack of belief in the idea that we can succeed or having a poor opinion of ourselves, even to attracting ill-health; e.g. minor epithelial tissue irritations on the scalp, or other areas of the body which reveals itself as a manifestation of an outward sign from inner frustration. We choose to believe in all or any of these weaknesses that form in our character and personality, which often affect our mental and physical health.

9

The Spirit of the Age

In our present social climate fresh forces occupy the market-place intent on falsifying information useful to the population and genuine teachings of a spiritual nature, bringing elusive distortions. These 'attacks' have one purpose, to cause confusion and weaken the moral resolve of the populace. We need to be on our guard. The Divine Books of the Ages all carry the same message, though it may be portrayed using different words; nonetheless, it is worth repeating: Those who fail to remember the God of all Creation, the Holy One, the Most High, rob themselves of their full potential. Furthermore, God's people are urged not to become conditioned to the world. To accomplish this the mind needs to be renewed all the time, not some of the time, since left to itself, the lower aspects of mind hold sway and attracts dark shadows; witness the mental aberrations experienced today.

We are encouraged by the Ancient Teachings to concentrate on what is 'beautiful and of good report' and not get so caught up in things temporal, because it is not through secular issues that we shall receive divine illumination, but through God's Grace which remakes us on the inside; however, our deeds and actions improve character and we should be mindful of this and do all we can to help each other. Hence the reason for a greater understanding of the self, coming together in a spirit of devotion, being of service to others. In such an atmosphere who knows how much the Holy Spirit will reveal His presence. Furthermore in this devotional atmosphere, the soul submits to the Eternal God with a deep desire and longing for Him and in these sacred moments the human spirit opens to His Eternal Influence, whose mission it is to guide the faithful into all truth, revealing everything the All-Knowing God wants us know.

In this hallowed atmosphere we sense the world's separation from its origins - God and why we experience so much fragmentation in our communities; the spiritual element is missing and must be restored, else we shall continue to 'do the things we ought not to do and fail to do the things we should.'

The Perennial Philosophy urges us to seek the Divine Ground of our being; but because of human short-sightedness it becomes foolishness to many, yet in all truth, proves the power of God to others. Time has shown that God's word is 'sharper than any two-edged sword' (Matthew 10:34); It divides those who hear it into two groups of people, the ones who perceive and believe and those who disbelieve. We have to make up our own minds whether or not God's word is true. Yahweh has said through the mouth of the prophet Isaiah:

> *'My word shall not return to Me empty; but it shall accomplish that which I please and it shall prosper in the thing for which I sent it'* (55:11).

Christianity teaches that all Scripture is given by inspiration – inbreathed of God – and is profitable for doctrine, reproof, correction and for instruction in righteousness (2 Timothy 3:16); though some will argue that much of the ancient teachings are allegorical. They may be classed as 'hidden wisdom' but can be discovered.

The sacred writings urge people to turn away from evil and ask for mercy. Pray that the life of the Christ Mind, which shows that it is possible to overcome primitive urges and allow higher principles for living to enter conscious thought activity, consume our will and so improve ourselves and the environment in which we live.

The times in which we live are changing. The world's social and economic climate speaks for itself. These are symptoms that prove the current system and policies are not working. It is time to heed the teachings of our former spiritual teachers, whose minds were guided by the ageless wisdom. For *'Prophecy never had its origin in the wills of men; they spoke of God as they were moved by the Holy Spirit'* (2 Peter 1:21).

It is worth keeping in mind that wherever we live on this planet we are subject to the weight of the oppressive economical beast, which has plundered many lands, adversely influenced wealth and resources; this was witnessed not only during the Lockdown due to the Coronavirus, but by greedy merchants and stock-piling behaviourism of some people during emergencies. If people would but pay attention to the influence of corruption, global financial contagion, the situation would ease and the people prosper. The light of God's truth makes a path to follow and the beauty of His Love strengthens our hand in adversity. Yes, there will be hardships to endure, but because of God's Love for His people the economic plight will pass. Our loving task is to glorify the one true God and we are promised that divine blessing will rest upon His people.

The OT contains many prophesies that were fulfilled hundreds of years later; such was the accuracy of some prophecies that one from the prophet Isaiah, (chapter 53) foretold the death of Jesus the Christ of God, with complete precision more than 700 years before the authorities in Rome crucified the Holy One of Israel. God's Word cannot be reduced merely to literature or sounds. The word is alive, active and gives life (Hebrews 4:12). It is effective to those who believe it because the Spirit is on the word. On the other hand it becomes ineffective to those who 'harbour thoughts of unbelief, unrighteousness, wickedness, hardened hearts and closed minds, not receiving the word in meekness' (James 1:21). But all that will change as men mature and the teething problems being experienced, give way to the higher thought processes with which men are endowed.

10

Knowing ourselves

The presence of good in a community becomes a public blessing, so everyone benefits. The spiritual element too expresses itself in a defining moment; unless the spiritual way is investigated we deprive ourselves of access to higher thought. However we define spirituality, it is my belief that it is the core strength of our innermost being and is so designed as to be inseparable from the three component parts which makes us human beings - namely spirit, soul and body. If we are sensible (and are able) we take care of the body, the word of God that we hear and pray about nourishes mind and spirit and the spirit in turn acts wisely on the soul. Why then is this pattern fractured in so many people? It is because men have turned away from God and are attempting to change His Divine Order. There are several reasons for this, we will consider the following.

Many people have unwisely yoked themselves to unbelievers and become deceived. Divine Scripture warns against doing this (2 Corinthians 6: 14). There are also certain individuals who experience a lack of harmony, not only with other persons, but within themselves, thus they experience warring factions within their own being. Furthermore, if the human spirit is weighed down by worry, sadness or distress it tends to become weakened and will fail to absorb the influence of the Holy Spirit, working through our spirit. This practice is not uncommon; unwittingly and willfully we are able to refuse the Gifts of God, but woe betide the man who does, he diminishes his own life.

Sadness of heart can also diminish our resolve to become more familiar with ourselves. We need to take into consideration the danger of attempting to reverse God's Order of things. We are seeing the fallout from this misbehavior in many nations. Another reason is that some people are apostatizing, they have put aside or lost their faith, as a result may fail to pray or believe in God.

A story is told in the Bible - 2nd Book of Kings (chap. 6) - of some folks in a place called Samaria (about forty miles north of Jerusalem), the city was besieged, a dreadful famine threatened the people, but there was among them a prophet called Elisha, it was he that secured their deliverance at a critical time in their history; what did he do? He prayed! The fervent prayers of the righteous – those who are in Christ - 'avails much' (James 5:16) and are a better defense than argument and all the violent behaviour, demonstrated by ugly crowd scenes, portrayed in the news media and TV screens.

Mary, one time Queen of England (1553-1558) is said to have dreaded the prayers of John Knox more than all the armies of Europe. To my mind men and women of God under-rate themselves; those 'in Christ' are the sinews, the bones and the muscles of a nation. Saints of God, arise! Be who you are 'in Christ' by:

- Obeying the teachings of Christ and the Divine Word, even if it opposes political correctness (but do not violate the laws of the land).

- Be willing to uphold the truth. Believe that God's Prophets were called by divine authority to teach, 'there is only One God'; be as They and remain in unity with each other.
- Be not of those who substitute the preaching of the gospel with human testimony; the testimony of the Christ Mind is the power of God.
- Follow the example of Christ. Jesus did not compromise with the religious Pharisees of His day.
- It is well to remember too, if we do not shape our own lives, we give others permission to do it for us, which is an abrogation of our responsibility.

Gaining Understanding

When men are more aware of their constitution and innate abilities, they will find unity is not so difficult. Each human being is endowed with a spirit of faith, which assists the human spirit and in turn the soul becomes acquainted with the divine mysteries and other spiritual realities. Our faith faces many trials, which we touched upon earlier, this should not deter the determined character. Indeed we should welcome it, since *true faith is proved only through conflict*. By its very nature faith must be tried, since it is the trial of faith that makes us spiritually wealthy.

All of us have faith in some measure; faith in good management, faith in common sense and in the people and things we see and trust; but who has faith in the Spirit of God, whom we can't see? Faith is a venture in the dark; we have to believe that God is good despite all that contradicts it in our experience; if our faith has been dislodged, the divine teachings urge us to get a closer relationship with God and lack of faith will disappear. A striking example of the trial of faith is found in the story of Job in the OT; it relates that God gave Satan permission to do what he liked to Job, but not to take his life; Job's story is horrific, but with all that happened to him, he never lost faith in God. By any standards that is quite an accomplishment. Sadly in our day, there is a fresh move to water down the faith in God or it isn't taught at all. This is nothing new, from ancient times God through His prophets has cried out against the so-called 'Under-Shepherds' who mislead His people.

The Christ Jesus said, "Love one another as I have loved you," Godly love never compromises truth, because it is the **truth** that sets us free from deception. Many people today are caught up in distressing emotional problems, unbelief and misguided domestic issues, all of which continue to be made worse by a weakening of faith in a God who is loving, nor revengeful. The various church denominations are not immune to difficulties either. Much of the conflict being experienced today is owing to some divines preaching 'another' Gospel and the ugly behaviour regarding matters of sexuality and racism. When the growing pains are over and men value spirituality as a means of education, pastoral care, secular and ecclesiastical management will be more accountable and trustworthy.

So many nations have compromised God's word - which would have kept the people on the narrow road - a word for which the Reformation saints willingly gave their life by being burnt at the stake, in order to uphold the truth of God's word, as many ordinary people, who love God, do so today.

We continue to see unrest and persecution in the Church and religious communities. The signs are clear - especially against those who claim to be of the 'household of faith', who have refused to hear the word of God and separate themselves from idolatries. Suspicion, fear, un-forgiveness, doubt and rejection are the weapons that cause division among God's people. The price of love is death to all carnal hurts and emotions. The Lord Jesus taught the truth and He was despised and rejected. He suffered severe cruel agony. Prior to His death He was separated from His Father, in ways which we need not describe in these pages. His sacrifice, made out of love for God's people, has opened the Gates of Heaven for all believers. This present life is a preparation for the one to come; when we follow God's Will our lives here will be improved. There is easy access to God's word for guidance, at least in the Western hemisphere, so there is no excuse. It is all a question of choice and everyone is gifted with this faculty, in a free society.

We are all under God's Edicts and the authority of His Divine Messengers. When we are rightly related to God we may claim the protection of Christ's authority over us. Nothing of what I have expressed is intended to offend anyone. I voice my views with humility, concerned for the Church I have served for many years. Clearly the Church is not in a healthy state. But these are just warning signs. What is to be done about it? The scriptures tell us to -

> *be anxious for nothing, but in everything by prayer and supplication, with thanksgiving, let your requests be known to God* (Philippians 4:6).

Everyone can do that! When things go wrong in any enterprise, management must take responsibility. Let Church leaders call all Christians – at several intervals - to three days of prayer, so that when God finally decides to judge the Household of faith, which He will (Acts 17:30) since we are in the last of the last days, that He will be merciful.

Pray too that God's Divine Order will not be tampered with any further; it is not too late, although a 'falling away' has been predicted (2 Thessalonians 2: 1-4). However, God has put the Holy One of Israel, in control. God is neither indifferent nor inactive in our day and is saying much the same as He said to the OT prophet Habakkuk, "I will work a work in your days, which you will not believe" (1:5).

In these difficult times we need a firm resolve to do all we can to support each other. What happens to one affects another, in ways we cannot always determine.

11

Do our Words Help or Hinder?

How much damage has been done by an unruly tongue? The Ancient Teachings inform us, 'The tongue of the wise uses knowledge aright' (Prov.15:2) This is one of God's spiritual laws and words guided by spiritual Law become spiritual forces working for us. Idle words work against us.

In the Letter to the *Hebrews* we read: 'He is upholding all things by the Word of His Power...' (Heb. 1:3). The scriptures teach that we should be careful about the words that come out of our mouth and believe more in what God's Word says, rather than our own feelings. Feelings change from day to day. The Word of God does not change. It stays the same, regardless of how *we* feel. In the NT we read:

> *'If you can control the tongue, you would have no trouble with the body'* (James 3:2).

Be not disturbed like nascent humanity, wrestling with primitive mind in tow, use your spiritual energies to guard against absorbing those influential attributes, brooding silently below. Be a trustee of God among His creatures and who knows what revelations will be revealed.

12

Apostasy

Apostasy is the falling away from the Faith. This happens for several reasons, one is that we fail to take God seriously; we treat His word as a smorgasbord, a salad to be picked over, leaving whatever does not appeal to the appetite. We shall consider other reasons later, but for now turn to Luke 14:27, 33. A distinctive mark of the true disciple is commitment to a Person - Jesus of Nazareth, the Christ of God. To be a follower of the Lord, Jesus laid down this condition:

> *"Whoever does not bear his own cross and come after Me cannot be My disciple ..."* (Luke 14:27).

Love without a relationship is like trying to be a Christian without going to Church. You can't be a Christian in isolation. I would encourage everyone to attend and support their local church, despite the difficulties you may encounter. There the Word of God can be heard and by listening to it, your faith will grow. Those who apostatise may find themselves on a slippery slope; so they need to ask this question: Am I a disciple of Christ or merely a church member?

To grow in love, Christians have to be discerning and avoid anything that dishonours Jesus, such as being exposed to vile entertainment which appears in the media. If what we are watching on our television (TV) screens makes us passive spectators, it is not Christian. Much of what we see on the TV is permeated by moral and spiritual impurity and has a defiling effect. If that is too radical for you, so be it, Christianity is a radical religion.

Deception is the greatest single danger confronting Christians in these last days; so few people realise this, which indicates that deception is already at work in them. Paul affirms this warning against deception (2 Thess. 2:9). Many Christians take the view that because a message from the pulpit is accompanied by supernatural signs, it must be from God. But this is not always true and may open the door to deception. So we do well to guard against that. One of the ways to accomplish this is to 'receive the love of the truth', which goes beyond listening to sermons, even reading these words, but calls for discernment and a 'revealed faith.' The Apostle Paul explains, "before faith (comes), we are kept under the law, until faith be revealed" (Gal. 3:23).

Where will the apostates go?

As Christians we have a message to proclaim, but it also includes pastoral care for our wandering brothers and sisters. Sadly this scenario has been unfolding for many years now. The scripture brings our attention to the seriousness of it. The early disciples voiced the view, 'where shall we go ...' (John 6:67-68).

The word 'apostasy' indicates a "falling away." The Greek word is 'apostasia', meaning defection, revolt; it carries with it a hardness of heart, which may be unintentional, but it attracts repercussions. Jesus spoke about it in Matthew 24:10-12. So it is important that we heed His warning and pray for those souls who apostatise. Why do parishioners leave their spiritual home? Another reason is the subtle influence of the widening crisis developing in Western civilisation between religious attitudes to life, on the one hand and a secular view of life on the other. To the thoughtful Christian observer, life is to be regarded sacramentally, symbolically, proclaiming some hidden truth and spiritual meaning. By contrast the secular mind tends to miss the metaphysical dimensions, the mystery escapes them and they fail to see through the window of the soul on to eternity.

Secularism tends to destroy the environment in which Christianity thrives. There is also a drive to break links with the past, indicating that a sense of history has diminished or at least is not highly regarded in today's society.

It is shameful that Christians in certain parts of the world cannot practice their faith openly. Furthermore, I sense that the dark side of secularist thinking takes the view, kill the idea and its purpose will be removed; this has been tried before, so Christians can take courage. Christianity has shown from the start, that the ways of God pass through the 'narrow gate' (Matthew 7:13) of suffering, humiliation and service and not through domination and power. We also have the Lord's promise:

"Heaven and earth may pass away, but my word will not pass away" (Matt 24:35).

Apostasy indicates a major shift in the spiritual quest taking place today, one which is moving from a less deductive to a more experiential method. Most people are caught up in these postmodern influences; it is not that there is an absence of Christian values, but rather how long will these values survive without the beliefs to sustain them?

Christianity emerged under the influence of contemporary Judaism and a hostile environment; the values of the Kingdom of God as expressed by Jesus and the disciples stood in stark contrast to the secular world. Indeed, at one time Christian purposes and practices were viewed with distrust and suspicion and its followers actively persecuted. However, once the Roman Emperor Constantine was converted to Christianity, in the fourth century, a different situation emerged. Christianity became the recognised religion of the Roman Empire. But it was not without its problems. There were those who believed that Christianity was being compromised and salvation threatened, which resulted in breakaway groups, such as those who withdrew to monasteries, to be free of corruption and power and follow a true Christian vision. Others, such as the Anabaptists, rejected the monastic ideals and found different ways of forming alternative Christian communities.

The early Christian Church was strongly opposed to secular authority, but the acceptance by the Roman Empire of Christian values changed all that and brought certain privileges to church leaders of the time, though many abused their position and this resulted in further divisions. But God's divine plan anticipated the threat of anything dire happening. By taking upon Himself our human nature, Jesus elevated that which was good, to a much higher level; His selfless action affirms the goodness of His person and the future of other humans and leaves room for elevation, making culture in society also capable of transformation. However, in view of the situation in the world, this transformation may have to be seen as a future event, rather than one that is immanent; though no one can be sure. God moves in mysterious ways!

We live in two kingdoms, as it were. The 'kingdom of the world' and the 'kingdom of God' governed by God and secular authorities, yet both kingdoms overlap and co-exists. This results in tensions as Christians endeavour to live in one and obey the other; but all the time we live in the world the place for Christians is in the valley, with occasional visits to the mountain tops for spiritual refreshment, essential for our health and wellbeing. Tension in such a climate is inevitable; struggle will result and may even be sacrificial in nature. I well remember how it was when I ministered as a street priest; numerous pressures were keenly felt as the dark side of human nature was expressed from time to time by misguided individuals, whose eyes were closed to the truth of the Gospel. I cannot say I was not nervous sometimes, but I put my trust in God and in what I was doing.

The impact of the Christian teachings has been a culture shock to many individuals over the centuries. This is understandable and we should not be in a hurry to judge others for their lack of insight. The disciples close to Jesus often failed to comprehend all that the Lord was doing (Luke 18:31). Like their forebears they had inherited and lived by the old Mosaic laws, that is until John the Baptist arrived on the scene and informed them of the coming Messiah, at which time they would be free, but free in a way they did not understand, because it had not been revealed to them. In other words, the men surrounding Jesus had not yet experienced the Resurrection, but when they did, a whole new world opened up to them; they were able to live as participants in the paschal mystery, i.e. in the death and resurrection of Jesus and when this is our experience, we too shall know the truth of Jesus' words, which is something to celebrate and be joyful about.

God's messengers – among them prophets, theologians, mystics, saintly individuals - boldly declare the message of the kingdom of God, without regard for their own safety. We recall the modern seers with affection and gratitude, men and women who have built on the labours of Justin Martyr, Origen, Augustine, Thomas Aquinas, Anselm of Canterbury, Martin Luther and Calvin, to mention a few outstanding theologians, who guided Christianity through some stormy and uncertain times.

The Church continues to preach the word of God. Furthermore, the Holy Spirit has been given to us as a gift of the last days (Joel 3:1-5) to set us on the spiritual path. Individualism is incompatible with Christianity and the pursuit of spirituality will destroy those tendencies; so keep on pressing on. We possess the Spirit as a member of the community and when He acts it is the church community that is edified (Cor. 14:26) so they in turn may pass on to others the fruits of the Spirit and be a witness to the glory of God.

Many individuals are unable to understand the Image of the Invisible God, the Radiance of God's glory, the Alpha and the Omega, the Incarnation, the Person and work of Christ, His pre-existence, His Godhead, The Person of the Holy Spirit, the power of forgiveness. These and much more have caused shock waves to unsettle the comfort zones of unbelievers and the rigid stance taken by those with more head than heart; as a result we shall experience their objections, so we should not be surprised, but continue to pray for them. Those working closely with the church are well placed to reverse the trends of the fragmented purposes of postmodernism and change its present course. It is time to forget the past historic blunders that Christianity has made; the injustices, violence and bigotry, in the name of religion. This only gives atheism, secularism and other faces of postmodernity an excuse to weave its objections to the Christian way of life.

13

Wellness Issues

In view of the devastating atrocities committed on this planet, we do well to become more aware of the wellness issues, which is everyone's concern. One of the principle topics most seriously affecting our health and the safety of others is the battle going on in the mind, e.g. the nagging thoughts of failure, inadequacy, a poor concept of self or a faulty ideology, which if allowed the freedom to roam, will so colour the thought processes, that stinking thinking will nurture the desire to either harm oneself or others. If not dealt with, will become a craving and those afflicted will experience its remorseless harassment, driving them to inharmonious behaviour.

The only way out of this dilemma is an improved understanding of the true self, a change in consciousness. When the inner self is renewed, the outer circumstances will change. The *desire* to damage must be replaced with the *yearning* to build. Creatures in the animal kingdom kill for food to eat. Humans kill to destroy and this is a primitive desire, which must be overcome if we are to make progress in this life and come together as a permanent unified community.

It is not a question of going soft on crime, which is punishable by law, but transforming the mind, so that the afflicted person alters his or her consciousness. A change in the thought processes within, one that complies with altruistic values, will alter behaviour and give birth to a healthier outlook towards all created things. Unless each individual addresses these issues for themselves, certain thought trends of a negative nature tend to inhibit creativity or cause the energies of the body to become unbalanced, leading to further unwanted tendencies.

Ageing

The ageing process is another issue that inhibits active participation in many activities. Ageing itself forms part of the human condition. If we fight it negatively we simply weaken our resolve to overcome and exhaust what energies we have. On the other hand, when one becomes ill and feels well cared for, recovery is more likely, a principle that has been known since the first physician took the Hippocratic Oath.

Modern gerontological approaches to the quality of life have advanced of late and appear to be well-balanced and informative, which avoids dwelling on the crisis situations to which many writers and news bulletins elude. However, we should take into consideration how agitated mental states get converted into biochemicals that cause disease and how the application of metaphysics is able to influence moods and attitudes.

Gerontologists might benefit from the age-old spiritual traditions that show how some individuals have preserved their youthfulness into old age. It is unwise to stereotype older people. However, a picture is often portrayed of the elderly wearing a mantle of sickness and mental deterioration, together with images of loneliness and depression; these physical and mental conditions are not confined to the older person, many of whom show extraordinary agility and mental prowess later in life, participating in various educational and sporting activities.

It is also important when engaged in any spiritual assessment, to strike a balance and remain focussed on the present task in bringing personal resources to ameliorate any problems at hand. A significant feature in health, spirituality and well-being is the implications of population ageing; according to a Global Gender Report (2009) the highest proportion of population aged 65+ will be in Japan, South Korea and Germany, owing to the fall in late-life mortality and the effects of the mid-century baby boom, especially in high income countries, including the UK and the USA.

The reader will realise that this information was gleaned before the advent of the Coronavirus, all of which has taken its toll, affecting the work of health policy makers, the food industry and Public Health Nutritionist in particular; however, it cannot be ruled out that positive aging may be more dependent on spiritual well-being than physical capacity.

Awareness of the spiritual process in relationship to positive ageing offers challenges and opportunities, including a balanced perspective on wellness issues, a sense of humour, internal strengths and resources for skills that focus on current capacity and chosen pathways, rather than dwelling on lost abilities.

Many of the problems that beset modern men and women today are similar to those in late antiquity, though social conditions were different, yet the human condition has changed little: people become ill, retain a desire to commune with the divine Ground and adapt to their environment; have children, work, nourish ambitions, deal with negative and positive emotions, power and status; they have a yearning for happiness, to love and be loved. To meet these needs the ancient teachings urge people need turn to the ascetic tradition, though it may prove a challenge to many.

Il-health and misfortune are part of life; whilst those determined to overcome explore avenues of higher thought, seeking principles that create a balance in living and an understanding of life; all live with energies they little understand and forces that work against them, because men have not learnt to work with them, though through improved education this is being turned around in many nations of the world, yet there is room for improvement.

When human energy systems are disrupted, i.e. blocked, or damaged messages sent to the conscious level of our minds that something is wrong, we need to address the imbalance before further damage is done. Energy systems are connected, e.g. they have a link between the physical world and the metaphysical or spiritual world and affect all aspects of our being. The same applies to our body, we are not three separate entities, i.e. spirit, soul and body, as convenient as this designation is. We were designed so that all three act as co-creators; whatever action we take, influences everything we are.

Anyone interested in wellness issues needs to be aware of the body energies through which the life force flows. It may be considered the greatest revolution of all time, which will free us from our unconscious impulses of lack and limitation, releasing us from any false hopes and expectations which might have contributed towards unhappy, flawed patterns which provide no real security.

There has been a cross-cultural awakening these past years which will eventually impact all species on this planet. Even now it is being felt by many people who are becoming conscious of the fact that the old traditions and the status quo of the so-called elite no longer serve the interests of everyone on planet earth. There is great abundance in the world and everyone would benefit if only all nations joined forces and pursued it together, instead of perpetuating the cycle of greed and destruction. Most individuals are able to absorb an understanding that reaches the cognitive and spiritual levels of the mind, knowing they have their origin permanently in God and are inseparable from this One Great Divine Mind.

When our hearts and minds are informed by knowledge and faith, we grow in wisdom and love. If through love and a more spiritual attitude men are not changed, can we say they have aligned themselves with the divine Ground of their being and know the truth of who they truly are? Spirituality is not a tendency towards piety, as if one does not have it in them to do anything wrong; rather spirituality is to be in possession of the life of God and if God is obeyed, this will turn men's souls from corruption.

The human mind in all its dimensions searches for meaning, purpose and a self-transcending knowledge, together with meaningful relationships, love and understanding; it is also affected by sad memories of the past, which can defeat our aspirations, e.g. when recalling a serious mistake or a bereavement, the same destructive hormones that caused the earlier stress are again released adding new stress, which is why psychology, metaphysics and good sense warns against dwelling on stored up emotions of the past and wanting to be in control; best to live in the present moment and draw on one's own spiritual energy, which through prayerful meditation increases our awareness.

14

We are here

This life can prove challenging, but we are here and depending on our disposition most find some contentment, even joy. Being here, we are to use what gifts we have, otherwise we falter and dark shadows cloud our judgement and reactions to our circumstances. The bottom line in dealing with our situation is our view of who and what we are; each person is a unique individual, with unrealised attributes, or as is often said: 'a work in progress.' The sentiments we have regarding the circumstances facing us are created within ourselves, not by others. Should we wish to make changes, best to start with ourselves, using patience, common-sense and courage. Dwell not on negativity, this weakens our productivity.

The needs of all human beings are the same, whoever we are. It is not our intention to comment on the sociological or economic reasons for existing disparity, these are widely known. Suffice it to say, many dear souls experience an emptiness that awaits fulfilment, which only the higher-self, influenced by the Divine Spirit within us is capable of satisfying.

In the days in which we are living, some are losing their capacity to relate to the Sacredness of the Divine in Creation. Contemporary research into the nature of consciousness reveals complex, mystifying, subliminal dynamics going on within the human personality and these hugely impact our feelings, values and perceptions. All the time society seeks to resolve their problems in the secular environment, human resources and man-made projects, devoid of divine assistance, there is little space for meaningful prayer or meditation. We are wise to seek the sacred ground of our being because in each individual there is a space that only God's Spirit can fill. This means engaging in spirituality or some form of religious belief, since such learning provides direction. Education, not blind faith reveals the truth and uncovers the wonders of the creation.

Seeking *God* leads to *unity* and directs us to love more deeply and improve this world. Then shall men see the power of love at work. It begins with each individual. First by casting differences aside, which are, after-all, only man made; e.g. Christians believe the Holy Communion to be sacred. If this forms part of faith then let Roman Catholic priests share the bread with their Anglican brethren and others, who desire to partake of it. God has called His priests to be shepherds and feed His sheep (John 21:17), not turn them away because they are different or not members of the same fraternity. Unity will prevail when men realise we all have the same needs, share the same aspirations for wellbeing.

15

Good and Evil

Few if any need reminding that evil is in the world and is perceived by the senses which can prove disturbing. However, evil was never a creation by The Almighty Loving God. In itself evil is the absence of goodness, as forgetfulness is the absence of remembering, darkness the absence of light and ignorance the lack of knowledge. When evil atrocities are seen or felt by anyone, these are the animalistic expressions of retarded humans, not the graphic picture of a being called the 'devil' sent to torment us. Evil intent is the responsibility of men, nonetheless, it impacts human outlook and leaves many bewildered.

It would take a heart of stone not to be moved by the plight of those many young children caught up in the awful atrocities taking place across the various nations in the world. History has a habit of repeating itself, e.g. the account in the Bible of the slaughter of many children under two years of age. This and other massacres perpetrated by evil minds see life through the eyes of dominance, greed and self-interest. Evil behaviour occurs when men exercise that aspect of the 'self' which harms or destroys the object of its evil desires. It is primarily a love of self and is a death blow to a righteous way of living. It thrusts aside humility, consideration, friendliness, joy, peace, gentleness and self-control - the *gifts of the Spirit.*

Few are willing to give their life to spiritual activities, though they be kind hearted individuals. Those who do not and consider spirituality to be of little value, fail to understand its everlasting worth. Everyone has their struggle with a turbulent mind. The issue with us today is not so much with external sins, as with the ideals of self-realisation. This more than our transgressions will lead us down a slippery slope.

Much of this attitude can be attributed to a poor image of ourselves. So many people suffer from depression, or lack confidence. It helps if we take our eyes off ourselves 'me' and look towards a more positive, helpful and hopeful outlook. A transformation has more chance of occurring and the individual will be set free of restrictive, inappropriate activities, because the hunger to feed false appetites will be replaced by the desire to understand our true selves, which always wants the best for us. The glaring difference between a person who acts justly and one who behaves with evil intent is that one acknowledges the Light within, the other rejects it. However, a fundamental problem for us all is the inner battle going on between the flesh and the spirit.

The Divine Books of the Ages, allude to this, e.g. see Galatians 5:16, no one escapes its infringements, it affects everyone, whether we're conscious of it or not. The spirit and the flesh are contrary forces, one preventing the other doing the things we ought to do. This teaching from the apostle to the Gentiles points to the flesh being at war with the Spirit and the Spirit with the flesh. When the soul acts without counsel or influence from the spirit, the outcome falls short of all God intends for our wellbeing. This to my mind is partly responsible for the problems facing society today; we ignore it at our peril. Nonetheless, it follows that all the time we are in this physical body, we shall experience a struggle between the flesh and the Spirit within us. The only escape, as the apostle Paul explains, is to *walk in the Spirit.*

More people have been brought low because they have held thoughts of doubt and remorse, dwelling on past wrong-doing. Indeed, we may have *sinned and fallen short of the glory of God,* but the way through this moral maze is a metanoia – a true repentance - the rest is God's work. By harking back to past sins, trying to please God, we unwittingly place ourselves under the law; but when we're led by the Spirit we shall not be under the Law. This makes no reference to the laws of the land; we all have to obey those! On the other hand we are mistaken if we think we can please God by pleasing men; this only causes frustration. We please God through faith, with the help of the Holy Spirit.

16

Freedom

Who can truly claim to be free when the world is guilty of so much uncontrolled anger, hatred, cruelty, greed and atrocities towards men and animals. We are free when we truly show love and protection towards all creatures; when we share what we have with others and ensure they have shelter and sufficient food to eat.

We are free when we protect the weak from the assaults of the strong and seek to unite, not dominate. We are free when we are true to ourselves and want the best for others. Men cannot be free all the time their minds are confined in a cage of unbelief or superstitions and false notions. They must be free to explore reality.

Our freedom depends on our dispositions, not our traditions. We shall be free when we share the worlds resources and help others towards greater prosperity; regardless of race, creed or colour. When all men practise altruism and learn to agree, overcome pride, corruption, greed, anger and understand the importance of keeping the ego in check. Only then shall we be free.

One is free when the heart and mind is attuned to all that is Divine; history refers to such individuals as pure souls. These are the men and women in society whose presence make clean the meanest, lights up the dark areas of this life, purifying the air in the most stinking of places. Our freedom increases when we have a better understanding of ourselves and this is an expression of our highest attainment whilst we occupy a physical body.

17

A house divided against itself

It may seem, to some, a tall order to expect all peoples to unite, but we are commanded to do so. Most welcome it, but regrettably not all. Can a person called to be a follower of Christ ignore our Lord's command to 'love one another?' Can a person claiming to be a Baha'i or a Buddhist, injure the life of another. Christians hold a special celebration each year for Unity, but how much unity is there among Christians? These words from the poet and Trappist monk, Thomas Merton are pertinent: "If we can unite in ourselves the thoughts and devotion of Eastern and Western Christendom, we can prepare in ourselves the reunion of a divided Christianity …"

God's household on earth is divided, there is little unity; the people are like scattered sheep. Many nations are in disagreement, indeed the behaviour of some is a measure of their ungodliness. On the other hand, there is some unity in evidence, but there is some way to go. Misty clouds of deception continue to form in the minds of men and the truth remains veiled from their sight; but God is not mocked! The All-Knowing *God sees the sons of men from His dwelling place; He looks upon all the inhabitants of the earth* (Ps 33:13).

It is time to make a more concerted effort to come together in unity, everyone will benefit. Why are men so blind. God is not impressed with the lack of unity among His people. In the Gospel according to *Mark (2:1-12)* we are given a good example of unity in practice. The friends of a paralytic man showed a unified effort in getting their friend into a house through the roof! the result was their friend was healed and their faith commended.

The Word they heard and the faith they held worked together and brought about healing; their friend was transformed. Their unified effort rode on the waves of determination. This story shows how working together accomplishes so much more. You might say they were *standing in the gap* (Ezekiel 22:30). Unity of the whole of creation has always been God's will. The patriarch king David, rejoiced that it was *good and pleasant for the brethren to dwell together in unity ...* (Psalm 133). Matthew's Gospel (24:10) also records: "... *because lawlessness is increased, the love of many will grow cold.*" This contributes towards the lack of unity among nations and people and many hearts are growing colder. Reverse this trend and we shall see a greater spiritual awareness in the world, leading to unity.

Main stream churches have made some significant steps towards unifying God's people, though there is some way to go. One of the problems that prevent Christians from 'holding hands around the Lord's table' seems to be one of identity, which results in churches cherishing their independence. We suffer a delusion when we think that independence makes us strong, it does nothing of the sort; it merely shows up our unrealised weakness. Our Lord was not independent of 'higher authority,' His life was one of complete submission to His Father.

Christians, under the guidance of the Holy Spirit can do much to penetrate the ecumenical impasse that has thwarted developments towards uniting God's people and do so in a spirit of love. The unity of the church is after all grounded in the saving work of God in Christ. Bringing the churches together need not deny their origins, language, history, customs and traditions, these things make church life all the more attractive. The time for unity is now.

God gave His Word, first to the Jews and then to the Gentiles, yet the rift between them remains. It is not our Lord's will that there should be separate families of God. Every effort should be made to heal the divisions that exist, since both Jew and Gentile believers worship and honour the one true God. The same can be said about the so-called 'separated' Christian brothers and sisters, divided from mainstream churches; it is time these 'broken fragments' were brought together and embraced in the name of the one Lord whom we serve.

It is also time to forget those activists who have previously persecuted Jews and break this vicious circle; also for Gentiles to recognise that the New Testament is for Jews, as much as it is for Gentiles. It is true that many Jews do not accept Jesus as the Messiah, even though the Gospel is relevant to them. Jesus was a Jew, born of a Jewish Mother, He grew up among Jews; His closest friends and disciples were Jews. The holy Eucharist, the Lord's Supper, is rooted in the Jewish Passover. Baptism is a Jewish practice and the New Covenant was promised by the Jewish prophet, Jeremiah (See 31:30-34).

If all peoples put aside their prejudices and searched their hearts, they should find no real objection in following the teachings of Christ and accepting Him as the Messiah, since His life and everything He taught is noble, honest and a saving power. Indeed the constant message of the Christian bible is that God provides salvation. Furthermore, God invites each person to discover their wholeness and freedom in close relationship with Himself; He also guides them from the place where they are. Indeed, the main theme of the Gospels is that God will deliver humankind from the misery of sin.

Morality and human happiness are inseparably linked with salvation for everyone, whether Jew or Gentile. God's salvation plan, unfolding itself in history, has a *unity* which was determined by Him from the beginning and which was to be consummated in Jesus the Christ. The Messiah Himself explained this point to two of His disciples:

> '... *how foolish and slow of heart you are, so unwilling to put your trust in what the prophets have declared ... then beginning with Moses, He interpreted to them the things about Himself in all the scriptures*' (Luke 24:25-27).

18

Racism

Racism remains one of the greatest threats to humankind, its underlying cause is first, antagonism between spirit and the soul, both of which are designed to serve the body. When the souls refuses to heed the spirit, disharmony is experienced in each human being, leaving the way open for unworthy thoughts, fuelled by fear and a lack of love and cooperation in human behaviour.

Racism is sparked off by the evil inherent in the hearts of men and the intent of those dark spiritual forces, whose aim is to implant fear and oppose the love of God and the acceptance of Christ returning in glory, as He said He would. When the higher mind dominates the conscious mind, the person acts motivated by the Christ Consciousness and not the lower self, as is often the case in our communities. Yet it does not have to be like this. By exercising the higher mind, everyone can rise above sensuality and view life in all its fullness. On the other hand, destructive emotions, taken to their limits are out to destroy. Of course we can say that about all the evil perpetrated by men. By using the term 'soulish actions' I mean to show that the actions of the soul are not the same as from the *spirit,* which in each individual relates directly to God, but the spirit also moves upon man's soul, the *soul* in turn directs the body.

Without the influence of the spirit, the unregenerate man is controlled by the three functions of his soul: the will, intellect and the emotions.

When the promptings of the spirit are set aside, this lessens its influence on the soul and so the inner harmony of man is fractured because the soul is no longer submissive to the spirit. Early Christian writers were well aware of this and wrote of it for our edification. King David – in the OT - expressed it in Psalm 103:1 *"Bless the Lord O my soul..."* When we view the world in all its reality, we see how important it is to find a balance between spirit, soul and body. This helps us to understand the foundations of racism, which is from one source only, the lower self (named in scripture as 'Satan.' Satanic forces set out to divide and completely destroy a nation. History is replete with examples. We shall recall just a few.

In the second century BC, the dictator of Syria, Antiochus Epiphanes, attempted by force of arms to compel the Jews to renounce their unique destiny as a nation and merge into the idolatrous culture of the surrounding Greek empire. It was only the courageous resistance of the Maccabees that foiled his attempt and ensured that there was a Jewish nation into which Jesus could be born as the Messiah. King Herod also annihilated all male babies, in and around Bethlehem, under the age of two (Matt 2:16-18); this evil act was prophesied by Jeremiah, some 550 years before the event. Coming closer to our times, the world is familiar with the activities of the Nazi regime in Germany, who attempted to disperse and annihilate the Jewish nation.

In His final prophetic discourses in Jerusalem, Jesus pinpointed two events which must precede His return to earth. In Matthew (24:14) Jesus said, "And this gospel of the kingdom will be preached throughout the world as a witness to all the nations..." Furthermore, at the close of His earthly ministry, Jesus gave His disciples an explicit command: "Go into the entire world and preach the gospel to every creature..." (Mark 16:16);

and in Matthew (28:19) "Go and make disciples of all nations..." all of which highlights the importance of unity in the community.

Finally, I draw your attention to the words of the prophet Joel (3:1-2), who writes: that at the close of this age God will judge all nations on their attitude towards the re-gathering of Israel in their own land. The words from the OT prophet are these:

> *"For behold, in those days when I bring back the captives of Judah and Jerusalem, I will also gather all nations and bring them down to the Valley of Jehoshaphat and I will enter into judgement with them there."*

If we have difficulty with believing in the spiritual approach in matters of Unity, the teaching of Paul to the Corinthians (1 Cor. (2:14), may help:

> *'The natural man does not receive the things of the Spirit of God, they are foolishness to him, nor can he know them, because they are spiritually discerned.'*

Once we have insight into this truth we shall love God all the more and desire unity,

> *'for eye has not seen, or ear heard, nor has the human heart conceived what God has prepared for those who love Him.'*

19

Guidance

Fulfilment in life comes with understanding. Lack of knowledge leads to impoverishment; no one can be happy when feeling a sense of emptiness within, which more often than not only God can fill. Besides common sense, we need the guidance of spiritual thought and science to guide our steps. Both provide a light that guides us to true ways of living this life, drawing us towards the fruits of contentment.

Most of us are absorbed in our own affairs which make many demands, leaving little time for the study of the higher influences of the mind, yet these too have a bearing on our well-being; e.g. what of the forming of *Cosmogeneses,* a term which makes reference to the creation of the universe and how it came into existence; it is a subject which profoundly affects everyone, even if people do not understand all the issues.

Whether we look out into the cosmos or peer into the living cell, we are conscious of harmony and order; to get the most from this study we do well to read and understand it with the eyes and mind of the inner (spiritual) self. It is not necessary to have a scientific or religious education to know that heat can cook or kill or that there is a First Cause,

An Absolute, The Uncreated One, A Universal Designer - which most humans call God and address as *Heavenly Father*.

A Living faith

As we move forward on our journey of exploration, we find that faith develops the certainty that Divine Power is active in the world. The old cosmology of Genesis and the miracles of the New Testament may not stand up to the light of modern scientific knowledge, but think of it this way: Miracles are the symbol – the language of religion. Mathematical equations, the language of science.

In a continuum it is not possible to conceive of anything being present which was not already in some form present from the beginning. Why should the dust of the cosmos manipulate itself so that it comes to control the very stuff of which it is made? The only reasonable explanation is that a Supreme Mind has breathed into chemical dust the 'Breath of Life' so that mind, working with universal laws, could exercise a measure of control over the cosmos and be guided by the will of God; who has done what the law cannot do (Romans 8:3).

Humans seek knowledge as water seeks its own level; therefore the conclusions to be drawn from the modern picture of the universe, point to a Divine Creator in whom believers put their trust.

20

Searching for God

The search for God is a desire deeply imbedded in the heart and soul of every human being, whether they are conscious of it or not. This yearning for the Divine sets us apart from all other creatures. It is a transcendental drive moving beyond the limits of our temporal fulfilment, making 'our hearts restless, until they find rest in God' - to use St. Augustine's well known formula.

The search for God has led people down many pathways. If we would know what God is like, we shall find enlightenment from studying the words and works of the Christ Jesus - His face was said to reflect *'the light of the knowledge of the glory of God'* (2 Corinthians 4:6). He impresses upon our souls the image of His holiness. Furthermore, our search for God leads us to repentance. This opens a way into the Kingdom, which has been prepared for those who love Him; but if forgiveness does not change us, what have we achieved?

The forgiveness of God means that we turn away from the old way of life into a new relationship with God, as Christ taught; but God's forgiveness will make little difference to the person who does not know that they need it. Confessing what is concealed relieves the mind, whether it is in private moments with God or to a loving, understanding friend. As we experience the unfathomable forgiveness of God for our wrong doings, we are called to show the same forgiveness to others. God's forgiveness is the distinctive teaching of Christianity and the higher religions.

Searching for God presents us with an enigma. We have been made by God, we hope for Him whilst we live, yet all the time we remain attached to sensual cravings, we find it difficult to do so; we cannot plumb the 'depths, the heights, the width and the breadth' of Jehovah God the Creator of all that is, so what is to be done? Many prayerful people have asked this question. The answer is woven throughout scripture and is found *within* ourselves.

God chooses us, but also calls us. When we are open to His love, His compassion, His mercy and follow His chosen Servants, He comes when we least expect it and reveals Himself to us. It has ever been so. This is the mystery of Grace, the sharing of divine life, our moment in the supernatural; God wants us to experience the fruits of regeneration, healing and wisdom, yet we have the ability ro remain aloof to His precious Gifts.

In searching for God, we shall come across ancient teachings most of which are reflected in, or have their origin in the Old Testament era. Jesus quoted from the OT often; we do well to make ourselves familiar with these teachings, regardless of the 'mountain' we have to climb – and all human souls have a mountainous peak to ascend – our ascent is made easier when we find encouragement in God's Promises, found in both the Old and New Testament, which together with our prayers and close relationship with the Lord, reveals the nature of God and His abiding presence.

21

Reflections

Many people live their lives in 'a vale of tears' yet nothing stays the same forever. The higher consciousness, in each individual, reaches out for a brighter tomorrow; it can do so because within it are the seeds of fortitude and hope, strengthened by The Ancient Wisdom; this seed lies dormant in the soul waiting to be awakened. It is on this premise that we can draw upon the teachings of the Divine Books of the Ages and 'Seek first the Kingdom of God' (Matt.6:33), from such perception flows divine revelation.

Be not of those who allow past mistakes and misunderstandings to nag and go round and round in the mind, like an old video/gramophone record? What of the circumstances that proved to be daunting; the relationships that are no more, the loss of someone dear to us and those moments of worrying that drained our vital energies. We need to face these moments with courage and remind ourselves, there is no road back to yesterday, some things remain irreparable and there is little use sighing for the 'old days.' Should we not do all we can to make the present better than the past? I can hear someone saying, 'I resolved to do that last year, but bad memories keep returning to haunt me, how can I be rid of them?'

There is a way; the Ancient Wisdom informs us:

Forgetting what is behind and reaching forward to those things which are ahead; press on towards the goal ...
(Philippians 3:13-14).

This wise teacher says that we should *forget the past*, i.e. unwanted thoughts. If the shadows of the past keep returning, Paul tells us to *renew the mind*. How do we accomplish this? Every time unwanted thoughts arise in the memory it may help to reverse the process by thinking about some former pleasant experience. For example, the day you passed that difficult examination, the moment someone showed you true friendship, the birth of your first child or grandchild and so on -

Whatsoever things are true ... noble ... just ... pure ... lovely, think on these things (Philippians 4:8).

Think too of the interests of others; turn thoughts to prayers of thanksgiving and away from sin or mistakes of the past; concentrating on unwanted thoughts keeps them locked in the memory. Be open to the Higher Mind and focus your heart on love, forgiveness, peace and joy, the painful images will then have less chance of returning and as the mind is filled with godly thoughts, a hidden strength will emerge providing a renewed confidence and the shadows of the menacing past will eventually disappear.

If we try to forget the past in our own strength the process may harden the heart; forgiveness has the power to take the sting out of painful memories and transform the mind. Everyone makes mistakes; it seems to be a skill most of us are born with! The way to deal with these gremlins is to recognise them for what they are; repent and forgive yourself and others. Confessing our wrong doings has a cleansing effect and helps in renewing the mind, but be sure to confess, not merely admit, there is a difference.

Whatever method we use to confess our wrong-doings - and we are free to choose according to our conscience - if the confession is genuine and truthful a cleansing takes place. We may be *hard pressed on every side, but not crushed; perplexed and not in despair; persecuted, but not abandoned; struck down, but not destroyed* (2 Corinthians 4:8).

There is much to give our energies to at this present time. Foremost among them are the broken and stressed relationships and human needs. Those who are married for instance, may find that one of the greatest obstacles to a successful marriage is time; praise God for good marriages, but in all families, unexpected things happen and may have to be dealt with immediately. Usually they happen at an inconvenient time! Another obstacle in marriage is lack of communication. Nothing is worse in a marriage than the remorseless erosion of intimacy between husband and wife; if this is not dealt with the walls of detachment grow higher and make matters worse until the couple are no longer one, but two separate beings. All of this will have eternal repercussions, unless resolved.

Since we are reflecting on issues that profoundly affect our present (and future), we should not overlook the most important of these - our relationship to God. This is an important feature of our lives here on earth. We owe the deity our allegiance, our worship and all that we have. God is the key to the mysteries of the universe. When we get close to Divinity all else falls into place; but I should add that God is true to the laws of His own nature, not to our ways of expounding how He works.

Follow the ancient counselling, *'be transformed by the renewing of the mind.'* The Infinite Intelligence – God - calls us now and this moment is precious; now is the accepted time. If our minds do not aspire to heavenliness, the lower aspects of the soul dominate and lead us away from all that is good. Should we be going through a difficult period, go through it, but never make it your martyrdom. Dwelling on bad thoughts merely feeds them. We make for ourselves a canopy for the future.

Little has been nor will be said in this message about the *future* since I have no knowledge of it and there is every possibility that all our days are as one – the past and the future merge into the present. Only God or His manifestations see into the future.

Best use our time wisely. For too long now people complain of not having sufficient time. This opens the door for neglect of family and friends, ageing parents hear little from their offspring, friends are forgotten, many elderly neighbours left to fend for themselves. We have sufficient time if we get our priorities right. When these are flowing smoothly, unity will prevail, minds will be more tranquil, leading to an improved society.

22

The Poetic Pedagogic Approach

Calling the world to Unity

Unity calls deep within our hearts,
like a thousand breathless dawns all new,
encouraging us to live wholesome lives,
expressing good deeds and all that's true.

This ancient message, like sunsets of gold,
wrapped in music's sublime dreams,
are truths that raise us above stormy clouds,
discarding trials in running streams.

In this celestial pact lies an ancient lore,
showing that we profit from affliction
and as we fulfil God's grand design,
we grow wiser from conviction.

Wisdom says: embrace this communion,
for it contains all that is divine.
It informs the mind, there is a union,
when we respond to celestial design.

***

On an island set in the ocean, people
lived in discord, isolated from each other.
Without little warning a huge storm burst,
causing homes to shake and shudder.

The landscape turned dismal,
covered in a blue-greenish hue.
The birds had stopped singing
and the fields were lifeless too.

The sky in the west was darkening,
gathering black clouds in its path.
The sound of thunder grew louder,
as the storm summoned up its wrath.

The tempest unleashed its fury,
as folks battled against the wind.
People and houses were carried away,
the storm would not rescind.

Unity boosts a Community

Suddenly the elements subsided,
people reflected on the scene.
The environment in grotesque sculpture,
mirrored where these folks had been.

It all appeared so surreal, some
saw it as a message from Nature.
They agreed to share resources and
work together, now sooner than later.

They resolved at once to change things,
so they planned to meet
and together clean up the mess
which had been laid at their feet.

'We must bring an end to our separation'
and everyone agreed,
But it wasn't long before it split once more
and the people were in need.

A shepherd spoke: 'It does not have be like this,
the answer is staring us in the face.
Purge the heart of selfish desires
God will use this as a channel of His Grace.'

***

Togetherness in Creation

Our lives in this world are not in isolation;
every soul is wisely formed in a relation
which is endless, in its all-inclusive creation,
as are other worlds, in their cryptic formation.
Knowing other worlds are truly in existence,
men do well to be mindful of their resistance,
to the important task of responsible assistance,
in making this world more safe and consistent.

The Universe is infinite and other worlds produce,
yet no one knows the outcome, nor can we deduce,
how it is these unknown realms remain so abstruse,
to human observation; when shall we reduce,
our limitations and discover where and when,
other worlds are more familiar to our ken.
We are so engrossed with ourselves, how then
shall we solve these mysteries which satisfy all men.

This life is harsh, yet exciting, but is not a game;
the world is changing, it does not stay the same.
Instead of brawling partners and passing the blame,
when will men unite and praise the Creators Name.
Perchance theology, philosophy and science,
will work in harmony and merge their reliance;
circumventing any form of pseudoscience,
since this would prove an appalling defiance.

Unity boosts a Community

Men of intelligence are keenly endowed
and know that truth is concealed by a cloud
of bias, ignorance and confusion. Some are proud;
such blemished notions in science are not allowed.
So for the sake of the people living today
and those generations coming our way,
it behoves everyone to take time and pray,
that revelation will help us make some headway.

***

If because of Lockdown you are
troubled with sadness or despair,
rejoice, we have within us resources,
which used wisely makes us more aware,
of our inner assets and properties,
which helps us to repair;
these may have remained hidden,
but have always been there.

Allow inner resources to express a
desire to create.
The ill feelings we find disturbing
will begin to deflate;
let not the experience disturb our hearts,
we shall grow in rapport
and emerge from this trauma,
much wiser than bef<u>o</u>re.

***

The Friend

A man went looking for his friend
knowing he had lost his way.
He searched the barren places
where the lost sometimes stray.

He walked along the byways,
searching every cubbyhole,
In his bag he carried water,
to quench the weary soul.

He saw the homeless people,
sleeping rough on the ground,
some in shop doorways,
in alcohol were drowned.

He wept to see the people
in such a sorry plight,
and vowed to continue searching,
all through the night.

Then suddenly it dawned on him,
this was a common trend
and every man he met that day,
truly was his friend.

***

Unity boosts a Community

Planet Earth

This world is but a reflection of a
much greater domain,
but whilst it is our home, we have a duty
to care for its creatures and terrain.

We are made earth's custodians,
to prevent whilst we're here,
any neglect of even a fragment,
in the human atmosphere.

This grave responsibility all
humans must assume.
As guardians of this province,
do all we can to make it bloom;

Protect the oceans,
the rivers, the lakes
and the meadows,
do whatever it takes.

Cleanse the environment of plastic
rubbish and all that's obscene,
Check carefully those areas where
humans may have been.

All this will be accomplished,
when men come together in unity.
By sharing human resources,
this will be our guarantee.

***

God's Worlds

Beyond this earth,
way past the skies,
are other worlds,
hidden from our eyes.

The One who created
all these spheres,
performed the task
with no false veneers.

All creation has a purpose,
which fulfils God's Plan,
for every living creature,
child, woman and man.

Let not disasters
spoil the good we seek,
nor destroy our hopes
or the way we speak;

For concealed within
our very soul,
are skills that enrich
the human's role.

Unity boosts a Community

These are ours, though
at different degrees,
yet the potential is there,
to develop most of these.

This world is our temporary home,
things are not yours or mine.
We are to share and prepare,
until called to a world beyond our time.

***

Composure

When humans live in harmony
with the divine nature of things,
we shall minimise the problems
which our craving nature brings;

As it is we yearn for excitement
and inflict upon ourselves,
chronic anxiety over possessions,
riches, fame, which overwhelms.

As higher sentient creatures,
we have the knowledge to amend
these misguided features, which if
not altered, will continue to offend.

***

Unity boosts a Community

Seeking Unity

Unity calls us to harmonise with laws
that govern life on earth.
Much like the breathless dawn of morning,
or a mother giving birth.

Men are not called to disputation,
but to a unified eternal Cause.
If we continue hostile conflicts,
we inject weak human flaws.

It does not take a philosopher, mystic,
or poet, to analyse human maladies.
Men can work it out for themselves
and return to truthful actualities.

There is much to discover in this world,
which to us seems new,
but without unity, we miss opportunities,
that makes our life fresh as morn' dew;

Could we wrap our thoughts and ways
in sunshine's brightest beams,
we'd see many conflicts disappear,
revealing human life is not what it seems;

We'd renew the pact of ancient lore
and profit from affliction,
fulfilling God's grand design,
growing wiser from conviction.

***

Oneness on the Planet Earth

It may seem a tall order
to want unity on earth,
especially since diversity
has been with us since birth;

There are the warring factions,
for which many men are craving,
oneness does not tolerate
that costly way of behaving.

The concept of Oneness
is a notion long desired,
by those who walk the path of
God, by whom they are inspired.

The oneness of the nations too,
fall in this same category.
Though men try to launch their plans,
none cannot ever become statutory;

For Oneness is born of a heart on fire
for God's eternal purpose.
Enduring Unity will fade away,
if there is a need to purchase.

Unity boosts a Community

Divine Laws were offered freely
out of love divine,
for the inhabitants of this earth,
to liberally consign.

As we gaze upon this world today,
Oneness seems so far away.
But the minds of men will not always be,
divorced for ever from fidelity.

***

A Panacea for Inner Turmoil

Harsh inner thoughts disturb
our very best intention.
A recipe extolled by the poets,
helps prevent their intervention:

Gaze quietly at a rainbow,
through the gentle rain;
listen to a blackbird sing,
its melodious refrain.

Whilst mildly forlorn,
a robin's plaintive phases,
may deepen our mood, until
the nightingale amazes.

Watch a glowing sunset
in the western sky,
or marvel at shooting stars,
passing swiftly on high.

Touch a delicate snowflake
from heights that appear grand
and watch it disappear,
as its image melts in your hand.

Unity boosts a Community

Have you been the recipient,
of someone's kindly deed,
or helped another person,
urgently in need?

It's on this spot where we live,
that we make the changes,
to improve our lives and character,
in steady decisive stages.

The time will come as we mature
and future challenges emerge,
we shall dissipate their influence
and old habits we shall purge.

The unifying of our senses
pacify our soul's desire.
When peace descends and calms our mind,
it helps our thoughts rise higher.

***

The Poetic Pedagogic Approach

Everyone has a Mountain

Everyone has a mountain
each one has to climb.
Some are more difficult than others,
but the ascent must be made sometime.

The years come and go so quickly,
many put the decision off,
yet there's a time and place for everything,
though the going may get tough;

Some say, 'perhaps I'll start tomorrow,
I've got so much to do today.'
Tomorrow, dear friend is a mystery,
Carpe Diem – seize the day.

Youthful vigour does not last forever,
all too soon we are in our prime,
absorbed in many duties,
with little time, to make the climb;

As old age approaches
and our hair turns white as snow,
we discover we're not so able,
the body aches and the gait is slow.

Shall we then gaze at our mountain?
which has never moved away?
And regret not having tried to climb,
when we had the chance one day?

***

Unity boosts a Community

Relationships

Relationships are often challenging,
though all are not the same.
For some folks, it's loving and serious,
to others it's just a game.

True love and unity is the answer
in every coalition,
if not present, it may increase
unwanted imposition.

Build relationships on a rock,
otherwise when it rains,
sorrow and pain become our companions,
these form mental chains.

No one willingly wants to experience,
familial devastation.
Make amends, become good friends,
before there's a cessation.

Such experiences merely leave a trail
of grief and sorrow.
We all need to come to terms, make
amends, before the dawn of tomorrow.

***

Caring Friends

Caring for others upholds a Community
and blesses all creatures on earth.
It encourages those with problems,
regardless of status or birth.

When the progress we desire for ourselves,
include the hopes and desires of others,
a Community will grow and prosper,
we'll live like true sisters and brothers.

Good people tend to show kindness
and are selfless from the start;
they love, give and care for others,
the result of a generous heart.

When you hear the words: 'I love you'
they mean every word they say.
If you're feeling lonely or wanting,
they'll make provision for you each day;

yet they too have their problems,
with which to contend.
When they put them aside to help you,
you'll know you have a friend.

***

Unity boosts a Community

The Unifying Light

From the darkness and the chaos,
came a Light to dispel human fears,
bringing joy, peace and unity,
to allay sorrowful tears.

This bright Light was once
depicted, as a luminous star.
calling wise men from other nations,
guiding science from afar.

Christ's story did not end there,
God had much more in mind.
He would send other Prophets,
to guide and educate humankind.

Let not clouds of superstition
or the traditions of men,
stultify the senses,
though men will try again –

by plunder and violence to
extinguish the Light, in the earthly camp.
Yet these foolish efforts will fail, for
adversity is the oil that feeds the lamp.

The Poetic Pedagogic Approach

In every age other Prophet's came,
with a distinct message for the season.
They taught unity and divine Law,
educating human reason.

They each brought a fresh portion,
of the healing Light of God,
liberating men from darkness,
easing the sting of the earthly rod.

Now men have no excuse,
not to come together in unity.
These ancient teachings, when applied,
will put an end to social lunacy.

***

Seeking Reality

Can a thousand sunsets wrapped in gold
melt a million snowflakes all ice cold.
What of those breathless dawns all new,
that makes the earth fresh with morn' dew?

Some long to live in this fragrant scene,
but for many it's just a burnt-out dream.
Yet beneath the silent stars high in the sky,
we seek life's meaning and wonder why.
He who has not cried tears to get his bread,
or spent lonely hours on his bed.
He who has never fought pain or hunger,
knows not the anguish that burns asunder;

Many people have been in a desolate place,
seeking harmony among the human race.
Only truth explains what it all means,
for this life is not all it seems.

***

A Gentle Reminder to us All

When gold is cast in the furnace
it turns red, yellow and bright.
Do not fear the ravenous fire,
it must shed its burning light.

Our gold will return more priceless,
free from all earthly stain,
when it's severely tried by fire;
no one lives without pain.

In the exhausting fires of sorrow,
each person yearns for release.
Maintain a positive attitude,
this distress will soon cease.

Believe in the life God gave us,
which in times may prove severe.
trials of life are taxing,
young and old must persevere.

Life's sorrows will always be present,
we must go through the cleansing heat.
It's in the furnace of the living flames,
these trials we must defeat.

Bear afflictions with patience,
let separateness be forgot.
We are in this life together,
ignore it, we cannot.

***

Summary

We have attempted to show that without an adequate knowledge of ourselves our human survival is threatened. It is imperative that we gain spiritual insights and an awareness of consciousness and basic scientific principles as they apply to our well-being. We have been educated to think of ourselves as individuals, which in a sense we are, but in reality are one and related. Unity does not mean sameness, but an integrated whole, since we are composed of the same elements that make us human, sharing the same capacities to know and understand, to love and be loved, to exercise our willpower and so on. We each go through the same life processes; we are all unique, yet think, feel and act differently.

We shall avoid the pitfalls of disunity when we recognise the fundamental oneness of the human race and our interdependence with each other and Nature. The Christian teachings, those of the Buddha and other world religions, including Spirituality, make a strong case to support this argument. Unity, therefore requires us to see that we are one and have the same needs and share the resources of this planet. It requires us to care for the welfare of all people regardless of their nationality, race, creed, class, or their other unique characteristics. Unity demands that we develop a global consciousness. It calls for actions that are universal, just and fair in their application. Once we see that unity is more than a code of ethics, it will be evident that civilization is poorer without the achievement of unified cooperation.

The sooner the peoples of the world extol the virtues of unity, the sooner a brighter light will emerge in the dark regions of the minds of all people and the nations of the world. The people of this planet have been separated long enough; the inescapable truth is that the modern world is in need of unity. If institutions such as the church remain divided, how can we expect society and families to halt the fragmentation of its unit? Christ's prophesy in Matthew (24:10) is again coming true: "... *because lawlessness is increased, the love of many will grow cold.*" One does not have to look far, anger, verbal and physical violence is increasing in our communities. There is an increase in apostasy, disparity is widespread. Reverse this trend and we shall see more love, a greater spiritual awareness among the people and unity will prevail.

References

Abdu'l-Bahá (1911). *Paris Talks,* Baha'i Publishing (2006), Wilmette, Il. USA.

Bahá'u'lláh, *Epistle to the Son of the Wolf,* Transl. Shoghi Effendi. Baha'i Publishing Trust, Wilmette, Il. USA

Harrington, A. (2008). *The Cure Within,* A History of Mind-Body Medicine,' W. W. Norton & Company, NY, USA.

Nabil-A'zam (1932), *The Dawn Breakers*, Transl. and Ed. Shogi Effendi. Baha'i Publishing, Wilmette, USA.

www.ingramcontent.com/pod-product-compliance
Lightning Source LLC
Chambersburg PA
CBHW021428070526
44577CB00001B/108